SKITS & STUFF

20 EVANGELISTIC SKITS FOR CHILDREN

DWIGHT HEIST

WESTBOW
PRESS
A DIVISION OF THOMAS NELSON
& ZONDERVAN

Scriptures taken from the Holy Bible, New International Version®, NIV®. Copyright © 1973, 1978, 1984, 2011 by Biblica, Inc.™ Used by permission of Zondervan. All rights reserved worldwide. www.zondervan.com The "NIV" and "New International Version" are trademarks registered in the United States Patent and Trademark Office by Biblica, Inc.™

WestBow Press books may be ordered through booksellers or by contacting:

WestBow Press
A Division of Thomas Nelson & Zondervan
1663 Liberty Drive
Bloomington, IN 47403
www.westbowpress.com
1 (866) 928-1240

ISBN: 978-1-4908-8445-5 (sc)
ISBN: 978-1-4908-8446-2 (e)

Print information available on the last page.

WestBow Press rev. date: 09/17/2015

CONTENTS

PREFACE

As a Bible teacher of school-age children, I have the privilege and challenge to present God's Word on a consistent basis that will get the attention of the students and teach them to understand and apply what they have learned to their lives. I have taught Bible classes for more than thirty years in different venues and in situations requiring various methodologies. But one thing is constant: the Word of God is unparalleled, and its precepts remain unchanged year after year. The message of redemption through Jesus Christ is timeless, as true today as it was centuries ago.

Children today face new societal pressures and are placed in riskier circumstances than most children in past years, including and when I was growing up. With each year that passes, it seems kids are exposed to more and more ungodly influences in our society. It is with this in mind that I have a burden for the Lord to work in the hearts of the children within my sphere of influence. When we have the privilege of presenting the gospel of Jesus to the kids in our church services, Sunday schools, and other gatherings, we can honor the Lord by preparing ourselves with the most interesting and well-planned lessons possible. For this reason, I have compiled this teaching resource of skits, plays, and lessons.

My hope is that you find this resource useful in capturing the attention of the children you teach. I would be remiss if I did not make it clear that despite our best efforts to be accurate and creative in the handling of God's Word, only when you cover each lesson you present in prayer will the Holy Spirit work to save souls and change lives. It is not we who do the work but the Holy Spirit of God to let Jesus change young lives.

AGAINST ALL ODDS

Will need—3 × 5 card and a pencil for each student.

After this, the Moabites and Ammonites with some of the Menuites came to make war on Jehoshaphat, "A vast army" is coming against you from Edom, from the other side of the sea. It is already in Hazazon Tamar (that is En Gedi). Alarmed, Jehoshaphat resolved to inquire of the Lord, and he proclaimed a fast for all Judah. The people of Judah came together to seek help from the Lord; indeed they came from every town in Judah to seek him. Then Jehoshaphat stood up in the assembly of Judah and Jerusalem at the temple of the Lord in the front of the new courtyard and said: "O Lord, God of our Fathers, are you not the God who is in heaven? You rule over all the kingdoms of the nations. Power and might are in your hand and no one can withstand you. O our God, did you not drive out the inhabitants of this land before your people Israel and give it forever to the descendants of Abraham your friend? They have lived in it and have built in it a sanctuary for your Name, saying, 'If calamity comes upon us, whether the sword of judgment, or plague or famine, we will stand in your presence before this temple that bears your Name and will cry out to you in our distress, and you will hear us and save us.' But now here are men from Ammon,

Moab and Mount Seir, whose territory you would not allow Israel to invade when they came from Egypt; so they turned away from them and did not destroy them. See how they are repaying us by coming to drive us out of the possession you gave us as an inheritance. O our God, will you not judge them? For we have no power to face this vast army that is attacking us. We do not know what to do, but our eyes are upon you." All the men of Judah with their wives and children and little ones, stood there before the Lord. Then the Spirit of the Lord came upon Jahaziel ... as he stood in the assembly. He said; "Listen, King Jehoshaphat and all who live in Judah and Jerusalem! This is what the Lord says to you: 'Do not be afraid or discouraged because of this vast army. For the battle is not yours, but God's. Tomorrow march down against them. They will be climbing up by the Pass of Ziz, and you will find them at the end of the gorge on the Desert of Jeruel. You will not have to fight this battle. Take up your positions; stand firm and see the deliverance of the Lord will give you, O Judah and Jerusalem. Do not be afraid; do not be discouraged. Go out to face them tomorrow, and the Lord will be with you.'" Jehoshaphat bowed with his face to the ground, and all the people of Judah and Jerusalem fell down in worship before the Lord. Then some Levites from the Korahites stood up and praised the Lord, the God of Israel, with a very loud voice. Early in the morning they left the Desert of Tekoa. As they set out, Jehoshaphat stood and said, "Listen to me, Judah and people of Jerusalem! Have faith in the Lord your God and you will be upheld; have faith in the prophets and you will be successful. After consulting the people, Jehoshaphat appointed men to sing to the Lord and to praise him for the splendor of his holiness as they went out at the head of the army, saying: 'Give thanks to the Lord for his love endures forever.'" As they began to sing and praise, the Lord set ambushes against the men of Ammon and Moab and Mount Seir who were invading Judah, and they were defeated. The men of Ammon and Moab rose up against the men of Mt. Seir to destroy and annihilate them. After they finished slaughtering the men from Seir, they helped one another. When the men of Judah came to the place that overlooks the desert and looked toward the vast army, they saw only dead bodies on the ground; no one had escaped. So Jehoshaphat and his men went to carry off their plunder, and they found among them a great amount of equipment and clothing and also lost articles of value—more than they could take away. There was so much plunder that it took three days to collect it. On the fourth day they assembled in the valley of Beracah to this day. Then by Jehoshaphat, all the men of Judah and Jerusalem returned joyfully to Jerusalem, for the Lord had given them cause to rejoice over their enemies. They entered Jerusalem and went to the temple of the Lord with harps and lutes and trumpets. The fear of the Lord came upon all the kingdoms and the countries when they heard how the Lord had fought against the enemies of Israel. And the kingdom of Jehoshaphat was at peace, for his God had given him rest on every side. (2 Chronicles 20:1–29)

Have you ever felt like an army was coming to threaten you or your family? An "army" could be in the form of sickness, financial distress, relationship problems, loss of a job, problems with learning, or any number of things. All of us have felt overwhelmed at some time or another and did not know how we would get through a situation.

What can we learn about King Jehoshaphat when Judah was threatened with annihilation? Prior to the account we just read, we can see Jehoshaphat was made aware of the great wickedness among the people and their need to repent, to turn from their evil ways. Jehoshaphat realized their desperate situation and ordered the people to pull down their idols and seek God. Also the leader of the Israelites, Jehoshaphat humbled himself in prayer before the Lord, asking for his guidance and mercy. All the people were in agreement and bowed down in worship before God. As we continue to read, we see God instructs the people to march to the end of the gorge in the desert of Jeruel. The people, who did follow God's instructions, did not even need to fight a battle but take their positions and stand firm to see the Lord work a miracle on their behalf. As frightening and illogical as the people must have thought this was, God tells them in 2 Chronicles 20:17, "Do not be afraid, do not be discouraged, go out to free them tomorrow, and the Lord will be with you." In faith and confidence in what God said, Jehoshaphat and the people fell down in worship before the Lord.

As we continue to read, Jehoshaphat and the people went to the assigned place the next day to watch God work. They sang to the Lord, "Give thanks to the Lord, for he is good, for his love endures forever." The invading army was destroyed in an ambush set up by God. When the people looked out over the desert, they saw only dead bodies on the ground and realized the Lord had worked in a miraculous way. The Israelites rejoiced and praised the Lord.

Each of us has circumstances in our lives that we mistakenly create or that we have no control over. It often seems we cannot overcome these problems by our own strength, but with faith in a great God, we can come through these times—if not find solutions to the problems. When we look at the example of Jehoshaphat, we see that with humbleness of spirit and a contrite heart, we can find forgiveness for sin and ultimately a relationship with this great God who loves us. First Peter 5:6, 7 says, "Humble yourselves, therefore, under God's mighty hand, that he may lift you up in due time. Cast all your anxiety on him because he cares for you."

God can work out even the worst circumstances in your life if you will just fall down at his feet and let him have his will in your life. When we follow his instructions through reading the Bible and praying with our mind on Jesus, ideas, strength, endurance, and opportunity will come!

Will you pray with me now to trust Christ as your Savior?

Pray a prayer of salvation.

Please take a piece of paper and a pencil and write down a situation you have had where God worked a solution for you and your family. Now turn that paper over and write a situation you are facing now where you need God's help. Put that paper in your Bible, and every day when you read the Bible, pray about your problem. But also thank him for answering the prayer for your old problem.

Remember this verse: "Cast all your cares on the Lord and he will sustain you; he will never let the righteous fall" (Psalm 55:22).

ALOFT

Set and Props—Chairs set up in two rows facing the front area with a worktable in the center. Drawings and posters of antique airplanes, flying machines and balloons. Hang model airplanes and gliders with fishing line from ceiling. Have a stack of paper that will be used to make paper airplanes. Place a sticky note under the seats of two chairs for student activity.

Characters—Orville Wright, dressed in nineteenth-century clothes.
Wilbur Wright, dressed in nineteenth-century clothes.
Jesus, dressed in biblical times' tunic or robe.
Nicodemus, dressed in biblical times' tunic or robe.
Facilitator.

Class enters and is seated.

Orville and Wilbur are at the workbench, making and discussing different designs for paper airplanes.

ORVILLE. Do you realize how long we've worked on wing designs for our gliders, Wilbur?

WILBUR. It's been a number of years, Orville. I guess it's good we get along.

ORVILLE. Yes it is. Now look at how I'm folding these wings on the paper glider.

(*Wilbur looks over at Orville.*)

ORVILLE. Do you think we can get enough lift for a twenty-foot flight?

WILBUR. Maybe, but we may need to adjust the nose a bit and widen the tail wing for more stability. Okay, let's try it! (*Take a paper airplane and fly it toward the back of the room.*)

ORVILLE. Wow, look at that. It was great! (*Turns to speak to the class.*) Hey, guys, how about if we get some ideas from you? Two of you have a piece of paper stuck on the bottom of your chair. Go ahead and look under your chairs. (*Allow time for students to look and retrieve notes.*)

WILBUR. Okay, let's both of you come up to the worktable to make your gliders. (*When they are finished, he again speaks.*) Now, let's see how they fly.

ORVILLE. We will start with you. (*Choose one of the students*). Ready, set, go! (*Let one student fly his or her paper airplane and then repeat with the next student.*)

WILBUR. There we are: two successful flights. Thank you for working on those gliders. You may be seated now.

ORVILLE. Wilbur, look at all these flying machines. (*He walks around the props and points to the various drawings.*) You know, very few of these actually worked.

WILBUR. Yes, it takes so many failures to finally realize the right design and combination of materials, not to mention proper atmospheric conditions. Do you remember all those summers on the Outer Banks of

North Carolina, the sandy dunes, wind, and storms? Finally, though, we broke through and built a glider that worked, and after that, we designed a steering mechanism in the nose and the rudder.

ORVILLE. It is an amazing thing to think of something invisible, like the air currents and the power of wind, can lift you and let the machine fly up in the air. It's wonderful, isn't it? The success we had in those early years of flight was certainly worth all the late nights and stormy weather.

WILBUR. You are right, Orville. All the hardships were worth finding the answer to flight, and it has been a learning and growing process ever since. Sometimes people overlook the power of the unseen, and they miss learning about truth. We have something so valuable if we know the truth and then follow up by acting on it wisely.

ORVILLE. Yes, we can have something beyond measure if we just trust in the truth.

(Orville and Wilbur walk from the room while discussing plans for their next airplane.)

(Enter facilitator.)

FACILITATOR. Who would have thought there was a day when people did not know what airplanes were? The airports we have and the travel that takes place when people fly from place to place or when cargo is transported around the world could not have been dreamed of at the turn of the last century, when the Wright brothers lived. After studying things such as flying machines, airplanes, helicopters, and spacecraft, and living with these in our lives, we tend to take them for granted. How many of you have put any thought into what makes the wings of the airplane lift the body of the plane?

Well, just as we become used to conveniences likes airplanes, cars, and electricity, we also become used to the spiritual blessings we have. God loves us and has blessed us with so much it is sometimes easy to forget to thank him. We are so fortunate to have the truth in God's Word, the Bible, where we can see who Jesus is and how we should live. The invisible things Orville and Wilbur talked about—the weather, wind, and air currents—are very important to successful airplane flight. The invisible, spiritual things in our lives are also so important to our functioning as God has designed us to.

Many of you come to church on a regular basis but do not put a lot of thought into it. Or you may take it for granted. At our church, we have many children's activities, camps, and study groups. Some of you may even be in a Christian family, yet it is easy to tune out the things of God, even when we are surrounded by them.

The Bible tells us in Deuteronomy 6:12, "Be careful that you do not forget the Lord, who brought you out of Egypt, out of the land of slavery." The Israelites were miraculously saved from slavery but soon forgot God and how he expected them to live and act. God had plans to bring them into their own land so they could prosper. But they took God for granted and had to learn some hard lessons so they could get their focus back on the God who loved them. Let us not get used to God and, therefore, forget him in our lives. The Bible reminds us in Proverbs 3:1, "My son, do not forget my teaching, but keep my commands in your heart, for they will prolong your life many years."

(*Enter Jesus and Nicodemus.*)

FACILITATOR. I am going to introduce you to two special people: Jesus, Son of God, and Nicodemus, a member of the Jewish rulers. In John 3 we read, "Now, there was a man of the Pharisees named Nicodemus, a member of the Jewish ruling council. He came to Jesus at night and said …"

(*Facilitator steps back.*)

NICODEMUS. (*Turns to Jesus.*) "Rabbi, we know you are a teacher who has come from god. For no one could perform the miraculous signs you are doing if God were not with him."

JESUS. (*Turns to Nicodemus.*) "I tell you the truth, no one can see the kingdom of God unless he is born again."

NICODEMUS. "How can a man be born again when he is old? Surely he cannot enter a second time into his mother's womb to be born!"

JESUS. "I tell you the truth, unless a man is born of water and the Spirit, he cannot enter the kingdom of God. Flesh gives birth to flesh but the Spirit gives birth to spirit. You should not be surprised at my saying, 'You must be born again.' The wind blows wherever it pleases. You hear its sound, but you cannot tell from where it comes from or where it is going. So it is with everyone born of the Spirit."

NICODEMUS. "How can this be?"

JESUS. "You are Israel's teacher, and do you not understand these things? I tell you the truth, we speak of what we know, and we testify to what we have seen, but still you people do not accept our testimony. I have spoken to you of earthly things and you do not believe; how then will you believe if I speak of heavenly things? No one has ever gone into heaven except the one who came from heaven—the Son of Man. Just as Moses lifted up the snake in the desert, so the Son of Man must be lifted up, that everyone that believes in him may have eternal life. For God so loved the world that he gave his one and only Son, that whosoever believes in him shall not perish but have eternal life. For God did not send his Son into the world to condemn the world, but to save the world through him. Whoever believes in him is not condemned, but whoever does not believe stands condemned already because he has not believed in the name of God's one and only Son."

(*Jesus and Nicodemus exit as Jesus continues to quietly talk to Nicodemus.*)

(Facilitator steps forward.)

FACILITATOR. Like invisible wind currents lift the wings of an airplane, so the Holy Spirit of God is like the wind that does a great work in our hearts—invisible but oh, so real. We know from reading later stories in the Bible that Nicodemus did become a believer in Christ Jesus. Nicodemus's changed heart was evident, because when Jesus was crucified on the cross for our sins and taken down to be buried, Nicodemus and a disciple named Joseph took Jesus' body and prepared it for burial. Nicodemus bought about seventy-five pounds of spices, myrrh, and aloes to wrap the body in, as was the custom of the time. If we read further in the book of John, we see that although Jesus was buried in a grave, he arose three days later, showing himself to many people. Jesus died for our sins but rose again and is alive. It is a miracle of God! This proves Jesus truly is God's Son, and as Jesus told Nicodemus in John 3, he loves us so much that he sent his only son to save us from sin and give us eternal life.

The Wright brothers knew their study of the forces of nature and the science of physics could help them produce a vehicle that would fly and change the history of mankind. After hearing the Scriptures that were read today, the truth of God and his Son, Jesus, would you be open to learning and making a decision to believe in Jesus as your Savior? God is invisible, like the wind, but he can change your life if you agree that you have sinned against him and want to trust in Jesus as your Savoir. Pray with me if you would like your spirit to soar with the Holy Spirit of God.

Say a prayer of commitment.

BARUCH WHO?

(Scribe of God's Word—Study of Jeremiah 36 and 37)

Set and Props—Room darkened, lit with candlelight and soft spotlights. Fabric panels hung and draped with dark-colored oriental rugs. Faux rock walls to a depict cave or basement setting. There is a wind-up mouse and a wooden box with a Ping-Pong ball inside to represent a large pearl.

Characters—Two scribes from biblical times in appropriate dress.
Baruch, the scribe of Jeremiah, dressed the same.

The scribes are quietly writing on scrolls with quill pens by candlelight.

BARUCH. (*Speaking quietly.*) Come in. Have a seat quickly, but be sure to stay quiet so they (*Points to the outside.*) don't hear us.

I'm glad you could join me today, so I can share with you the story of a very frightening time in my life. My name is Baruch, and my job was as a scribe. "What is a scribe?" you might ask. Well, a scribe is a professional penman who makes written copies of God's Word for others to read. You see, the printing press or word processor was not yet invented. I often worked for Jeremiah, the son of Hilkiah, one of the priests Anathoth in the territory of Benjamin. Jeremiah loved God and faithfully proclaimed God's Word for forty years while enduring beatings, opposition, and imprisonment. Jeremiah was often called the "weeping prophet," because he was of a sensitive and sympathetic nature. God, however, called Jeremiah to deliver stern warnings and messages of judgment to the people of Israel, because they lived in continual sin and stubbornly would not repent. Jeremiah started off his ministry when Josiah was king. What a good king he was. Later, after Josiah died, there was so much opposition to Jeremiah's message under the rule of King Jehoiakim that he wanted to resign from being a prophet, but he continued to proclaim God's Word.

(*Baruch looks through stack of scrolls.*)

(*Scribe 1 takes a break to get a dipper of water.*)

(*Scribe 2 stores his scroll, shuffles around, and bends down to place the wind-up mouse on the floor.*)

(*The scribes chase and catch the wind-up mouse to kill it and then go back to writing on their scrolls.*)

BARUCH. Here it is— Why … what is all this commotion? Scribes, you have many days of work ahead of you. Go back to work!

Now then, let me tell you my story. In the fourth year of Jehoakim, king of Judea, this word came to Jeremiah from the Lord: "Take a scroll and write on it all the words I have spoken to you concerning Israel, Judah and all the other nations from the time I began speaking to you in the reign of Josiah till now. Perhaps when the people of Judah hear about every disaster I plan to inflict on them, each of them will turn from his wicked way; then I will forgive their wickedness and their sin."

So Jeremiah called me to write on a scroll all the words of God. After God's Word was written, Jeremiah asked me to go to the temple, the house of the Lord, during a religious ceremony and read to the people from the scroll. You see, Jeremiah was restricted in where he went and was not allowed to go to the temple. He also prayed the people would turn from their sins after hearing God's Word and seek the Lord.

I followed Jeremiah's instructions and went to the temple. I read the words of God from the scroll. It seems the religious people did not like the Word of the Lord very much. I suppose they didn't want to admit their sins and change their ways.

Apparently some of the government officials heard me read at the temple, because after I read the scroll to the religious people, government officials wanted me to come and read it to the them at the official secretary's office. When I finished reading to them, I was told I would need to appear before the king. The officials looked at me with fear and told me they must report these words to the king. Then they said to me, "Tell us, how did you come to write all this? Did Jeremiah dictate it?" I told them he did and that I wrote them in ink on the scroll. The officials told me I needed to get Jeremiah and hide; I could not let anyone know where we were. That's why we started to do our work down here—hoping no one would find us. (*Baruch whispers.*) You won't tell anyone, will you?

Later that day, I heard the king ordered the secretary to give the scroll to Jehudi, a reader of the court, so he could read it to him. Well, as Jehudi finished the first column, the king cut off the scroll with a knife and tossed it into the fire pit. As Jehudi continued reading God's Word, the king continued cutting up the scroll and burning it. The king did not respond to God's Word favorably. He told his officials to find and arrest Jeremiah and me. The Lord, however, protected us, and we stayed hidden here. And even though the king was angry at the Lord's Word and the people ignored God, God's Word lasts forever. The Lord again spoke to Jeremiah, telling him to dictate another scroll just like the first one and to add the things that happened.

Sadly, because the people of Israel did not seek forgiveness for their sins, God brought judgment on Israel after about three months, and a wicked country overthrew their government.

I warn all of you here to listen to God's Words to us and know the path to salvation in your own life. Let me show you something. Now where is it? (*He looks around.*) Here it is! (*Baruch takes the "pearl" out of the box and holds it up.*) Have you ever seen such a pearl?

(*The scribes look up from their writing.*)

SCRIBES. Nice. (*The scribes go back to writing.*)

How expensive this must have been! Jesus can give us the new life we need, because God sent him to die on the cross for our sins. He died and then rose from the dead three days later, proving he is God! He is alive today and loves us. Believing and trusting in Jesus is the salvation we are talking about. This is salvation from sin, like Jeremiah was writing about to the people. God wants us to admit and confess our sins, believe what Jesus did for us on the cross, and then trust in him as our Savior. This pearl represents the most important thing in our life. In Matthew 13:45 we read, "Again, the kingdom of heaven is like a merchant looking for fine pearls. When he found one of great value, he went away and sold everything he had and bought it." This pearl was bought with Jesus' blood on the cross and represents our salvation from sin. God's Word shows us how to be saved and live for him! Are you saved by the blood of Jesus? Have you asked forgiveness for your sins and trusted Jesus to live in your life? Now is the time to do that. God's Words stand now and forever. They are true.

(*Ask for commitments to be saved.*)

CLIMB THREE MOUNTAINS

Set—One papier-mâché mountain, painted in neutral colors. There is a large papier-mâché rock next to mountain, with enough space to walk around each one. There are a replica of the Ten Commandments, a simulated "burning bush" (possibly Christmas lights in a shrub), and binoculars.

Characters—Hiker, dressed in hiker gear with ropes, canteen, climbing manual, backpack, etc.
Moses dressed in biblical robes with a head covering and sandals.
Narrator.

The class enters and walk around the mountain. Then they sit on the floor around the mountain and rock.

(*The hiker enters and speaks, walking around the mountain and between class members.*)

HIKER. I am having a real problem with all this stuff. It's heavy and bulky, and I can hardly move. That outfitter kept telling me I need to hydrate, need certain shoes, and this and that. This is no fun but just a bunch of rules. I thought this was going to be a hike not boot camp! (*The hiker sits on the floor.*)

NARRATOR. In Exodus 19:16–25 we read, "On the morning of the third day there was thunder and lightning, with a thick cloud over the mountain, and a very loud trumpet blast. Everyone in the camp trembled. Then Moses led the people out of the camp to meet with God, and they stood at the foot of the mountain. Mt. Sinai was covered with smoke, because the Lord descended on it in fire. The smoke billowed up from it like smoke from a furnace, the whole mountain trembled violently, and the sound of the trumpet grew louder and louder. Then Moses spoke and the voice of God answered him. The Lord descended to the top of Mt. Sinai and called Moses to the top of the mountain. So Moses went up and the Lord said to him, 'Go down and warn the people so they do not force their way through to see the Lord and many of them perish. Even the priests, who approach the Lord, must consecrate themselves, or the Lord will break out against them.' Moses said to the Lord, 'The people cannot come up to Mt. Sinai, because you yourself warned us "Put limits around the mountain and set it apart as holy."' The Lord replied, 'Go down and bring Aaron up with you. But the priests and the people must not force their way through to come up to the Lord, or he will break out against them.' So Moses went down to the people and told them."

(*Moses enters, kneels next to the rock and bows his head. He looks up and around and finds the replica of the Ten Commandments next to the rock.*)

NARRATOR. If we continue to read chapter 20 of Exodus, we see the Ten Commandments, which Moses brought from the mountain, read to the people. These are the rules set forth by God for us to live by. Or society's rules were based on these. US laws are based on the commandments. They include, "Thou shall not murder." We can base a healthy and moral life on these commandments. We should not feel like these rules are a burden. They are protection and good for us.

(*Moses exits, and narrator steps back.*)

HIKER. I guess the outfitter was right. I do need to drink a lot of water so I don't get dehydrated. Also, I need the ropes and stuff, so I can get around up here on the rocks and not hurt myself or get stuck. Maybe the rules are not so bad after all. (*The hiker starts to walk and pretends to climb, wiping sweat off his forehead. He slips on the trail and falls. He gets angry.*)

This stupid mountain! I knew I could have done better taking a shortcut instead of following the trail. What do the people who made the trail map know that I don't know? I could have saved a bunch of time and not almost break my neck. (*Tired, he sits down and rubs his leg.*)

NARRATOR. Let's read about another mountain in the Bible. It says in Deuteronomy 34:1–4, "Then Moses climbed Mt. Nebo from the plains of Moab to the top of Pisgah, across from Jericho. There the Lord showed him the whole land—from Gilead to Dan, all of Naphtali, the territory of Ephraim and Manasseh, all the land of Judah as far as the western sea, the Negev and the whole region from the valley of Jericho, the City of Palms, as far as Zoar. Then the Lord said to him, 'This is the land I promised an oath to Abraham, Isaac and Jacob when I said, "I will give it to your descendants." I have let you see it with your eyes, but you will not cross over to it.'" After forty long years of wandering in the desert, the people of Israel came to their own land, which God had promised them years before. Because the people had not trusted God to take over their land and its inhabitants, he punished them by not giving it to them for those forty years. Moses was allowed to see but not enter this Promised Land before his death. Only the younger generation, along with two leaders of faith, Caleb and Joshua, were allowed to enter.

(*Moses enters with binoculars as previous Scripture is read. He looks in awe at the Promised Land and then exits.*)

NARRATOR. God tells us in the book of Romans that we are all sinners, and this causes us to not have fellowship with God. God loves people but hates sin, and he has provided a way to take away our sins; that way is Jesus. Jesus died on the cross for our sins and was risen from the grave three days later, which proves he is God. Do you know Jesus? Have you asked forgiveness for your sins? There are no shortcuts to heaven. The only the way God has provided is through faith in Jesus Christ. The hiker thought he could take a shortcut to the mountaintop, but he was young. You cannot work your way to heaven by a shortcut. Only through belief in Jesus will you go to this wonderful place.

(*The narrator steps back.*)

(*Moses enters and looked around. Turn on simulated burning bush. Moses takes cover behind the rock, covering his face with robe.*)

NARRATOR. Exodus 3:1–15 says, "Now Moses was tending the flock of Jethro his father-in-law, the priest of Midian, and he led the flock to the far side of the desert and came to Horeb, the mountain of God. There the angel of the Lord appeared to him in flames of fire from within a bush. Moses saw that though the bush was on fire it did not burn up. So Moses thought, 'I will go over and see this strange sight—why the bush did not burn up.' When the Lord saw that he had gone over to look, God called to him from within the bush, 'Moses, Moses!' And Moses said, 'Here I am.' 'Do not come any closer,' God said. 'Take off your sandals, for the place where you are standing is holy ground.' Then he said, 'I am the God of your father, the God of Abraham, the god of Isaac and the God of Jacob.' At this, Moses hid his face, because he was afraid to look at God. The Lord said, 'I have indeed seen the misery of my people in Egypt. I have heard them crying out because of their slave drivers, and I am concerned about their suffering. So I have come down to rescue them from the hand of the Egyptians and to bring them out of that land into a good and spacious land, a land flowing with milk and honey—the home of the Canaanites, Hittites, Amorites, Perizzites, Hivites and Jebusites. And now the cry of the Israelites has reached me, and I have seen the way the Egyptians are oppressing them. So now go, I am sending you to Pharaoh to bring my people the Israelites out of Egypt.' But Moses said to God, 'Who am I, that I should go to Pharaoh and bring the Israelites out of Egypt?' And God said, 'I will be with you. And this will be the sign to you that it is I that who have sent you: When you have brought the people out of Egypt, you will worship God on this mountain.' Moses said to God, 'Suppose I go to the Israelites and say to them, "The God of your fathers has sent me to you," and they ask me, "What is his name?" Then what shall I say to them?' God said to Moses, 'I am who I am. This is what you are to say to the Israelites: "I AM has sent me to you."' God also said to Moses, 'Say to the Israelites, "The Lord, the God of your fathers—The God of Abraham, the God of Isaac and the God of Jacob—has sent me to you." This is my name forever, the name by which I am to be remembered from generation to generation.'"

(*The narrator steps back.*)

(*The hiker stands.*)

HIKER. I now see how spoiled and complaining I have been. I resented rules that are set forth for my benefit and wanted an easy way up the mountain and in my life. There are no shortcuts to the top. There isn't my way—just God's way, because *he* is holy and all-knowing. I need to submit to him. A friend of mine shared Joshua 24:15 with me: "But if serving the Lord seems undesirable to you, then choose for yourselves this day whom you will serve."

Have you been stubborn in your life? Are you ready to believe in Jesus and trust him as your savior? Will you follow the example of Moses and follow the path of God? Pray with me if you are ready to make a change in life.

(*The audience bows their heads and prays.*)

Dear Lord God, I have wanted to do things my way and not yours. I know

I am a sinner and am so sorry for these sins. Please forgive me through the blood of Jesus on the cross. I believe you came to save me from my sins and change my life. Please take me and change me. I trust you with my life, and I want to serve you. I love you, Lord. Amen.

COFFEE, TEA, OR ME

(A Study of How We Are Known)

Set and Props—There is a table with a cardboard sign on the front that includes a coffee shop logo or a sign on the wall. A blender, hot/cold coffee cups, napkins, straws, and towel are also on the set.

Characters—Barista, wearing an apron.
> Customer (s)—Same person may play all customers.
> Facilitator—Same person may also be one of the customers.

Costumes—Simple changes in costume for each customer, that is, hats, scarves, glasses, etc.

(*Barista enters and stands behind table.*)

(*Customers 1–10 will enter with change in costume.*)

BARISTA. Welcome to the (name of coffee shop). We are here to serve our customers, and we offer many kinds of coffee and tea drinks. I feel like I know the regulars who come in and order things almost every day. Sometimes I sit and think about what these people's lives are like. Then I think about what they order and realize this is what I see in them and how I know them. Well, I should not judge, but you know, when you see people and what they do, it seems that is what you think of them. It's a funny thing, isn't it?

BARISTA. Oh, excuse me. Here comes Mr. Mocha Frappuccino.

CUSTOMER #1. (*Customer walks to the counter.*) Good morning. I'd like the usual. (*He hands the barista money.*)

BARISTA. Large mocha frappuccino light, with extra whipped cream and extra mocha drizzle.

CUSTOMER #1. You never forget!

(*Barista prepares the drink and hands it to the customer.*)

BARISTA. Bye! Have a good day. (*The barista cleans the counter with a towel.*)

CUSTOMER #1. Bye.

(*Customer #2 enters.*)

CUSTOMER #2. I need a medium red-eye. Quick!

BARISTA. You didn't sleep last night, did you?

CUSTOMER #2. Too much on my mind. Do you have my red-eye ready yet? (*Customer #2 hands the barista money.*)

BARISTA. Coming right up. This should help you wake up. (*The barista hands the drink to the customer.*)

(*Customer #2 exits.*)

CUSTOMER #3. (*Customer enters and walks up to the counter.*) Large half-caf, skinny, hazelnut latte, please. How are you doing today?

BARISTA. Oh, I'm good. Is your wife feeling better?

CUSTOMER #3. She is, but still rather tired. It's a slow process. (*The customer hands a payment card to the barista.*)

BARISTA. Here's your latte. Enjoy!

CUSTOMER #3. Thanks. (*Customer #3 leaves.*)

(*The barista cleans up with the towel.*)

CUSTOMER #4. (*Customer enters and orders.*) Good morning. I'll have a large Columbian with whole milk. (*The customer hands money to the barista.*)

BARISTA. (*The barista prepares the cup.*) Here you go. (*The barista gives Customer #4 the cup and takes the money.*)

CUSTOMER #4. See you tomorrow. (*Customer #4 exits.*)

BARISTA. Oh boy! Here comes a complicated one. It's good I can count!

CUSTOMER #5. (*Customer #5 places an order.*) Hi! Seven-pump white mocha with ten pumps coffee, white mocha frappuccino with white mocha drizzle—no whip. Here's my card.

BARISTA. (*Barista takes payment and gives back the card.*) Okay. This will take just a few minutes. You getting ready for a busy day?

CUSTOMER #5. Very busy! The accountants are coming today.

BARISTA. (*Barista hands the drink to the customer.*) Here you are. Enjoy!

CUSTOMER #5. Thanks. Have a good day. (*Customer #5 exits.*)

BARISTA. Whew! We've been busy today, but I'm not complaining. Job security, you know. Oh, here comes skinny vanilla latte.

CUSTOMER #6. (*Customer #6 enters and places an order.*) Small, skinny, vanilla latte, please. (*Customer hands the barista the payment card.*)

BARISTA. (*Barista hands the card and drink to the customer.*) You have a good day now, all right?

CUSTOMER #6. Thank you. Bye. (*Customer #6 leaves.*)

CUSTOMER #7. (*Customer #7 enters.*) I'd like a medium dry cappuccino.

BARISTA. I'll get that for you. Are you on your way to work today?

CUSTOMER #7. (*Customer #7 hands money to the barista.*) Yes, I hope things calm down a little at work. I'm getting too old for all the drama.

BARISTA. Well, you enjoy it, and relax a little today, okay? (*The barista hands the drink to the customer.*)

CUSTOMER #7. Bye. (*Customer #7 exits.*)

BARISTA. Here comes my green tea customer, right on schedule.

CUSTOMER #8. (*Customer #8 enters and places an order.*) Good morning. I think I'll have a large, green tea frappuccino.

BARISTA. (*The barista places hand next to mouth and speaks to the *audience.*) See, I told you who she is! (*The barista speaks to the customer.*) Let me get that for you right away.

CUSTOMER #8. (*Customer hands the barista payment.*) Thank you. I hope you have a great day. (*The customer exits.*)

BARISTA. Thank you. Bye.

CUSTOMER #9. (*Customer enters.*) Hi! How are you doing today?

BARISTA. Oh, I'm doing good. Can I get you your regular?

CUSTOMER # 9. (*The customer hands money to the barista.*) Yes, the large, quad, cinnamon dolche latte.

BARISTA. Coming right up!

CUSTOMER #9. You always do such a good job on my drink.

BARISTA. (*The Barista hands drink to customer.*) Here you go. Thank you.

CUSTOMER #9. Bye, see you later. (*Customer #9 exits.*)

BARISTA. (*The barista puts hand next to mouth and speaks to audience.*) Oh, this guy always acts like he's making a big decision but always orders the same thing. (*The barista speaks to the customer.*) What can I get you today?

CUSTOMER #10. Well, let's see. I don't know what I want today. Let me think. Well, I guess I'll have a large, de-caf, soy, sugar-free, caramel, coffee frappuccino light. (*The customer hands the barista a payment card.*)

BARISTA. (*The barista takes the card and hands back to customer.*) Okay. I'll work on that for you right away. Here you go.

CUSTOMER #10. Looks good. Thank you so much. (*Customer exits.*)

BARISTA. Bye! (*The barista sits to the side.*)

(*The facilitator moves to the front of the counter.*)

FACILITATOR. You can see that at this coffee shop, the barista knows the customers by what they order. What do people know you by? Do you know people form opinions of us and think they know us just by looking at us or by our actions? We may think this is unfair, but sometimes our behavior and choices show who we are. If our behavior is bad, people think of us like that and may never change their opinion of us.

God also knows us, but he knows who we really are because he created us. He know us better than we know ourselves, because he even knows our future potential. Psalm 94:11 says, "The Lord knows the thoughts of man."

When certain customers came into the coffee ship, they were known simply by their drink preference. When people see your behavior, they also know you by it. For example, you may be described as friendly, mean, disrespectful, or as a troublemaker. And you likely judge your own friends, teachers, and others by what you see them do.

God does care about our actions as we read in Proverbs 20:11: "Even a child is known by his actions, by whether his conduct is pure and right. Ears that hear and eyes that see—the Lord has made them both." You might say you do not care how you speak or act, but as shown in the verse we just read, God does. You see, God cares about who we are and how we get along with others and reflect his love. God knows we are born sinners, and he offers us the chance to change our lives and be saved from that sin by trusting in Jesus as our Savior. When we are sorry for our sins and confess them, believe in what Jesus did for us on the cross and his resurrection, he will forgive us and we are saved. The change that can take place in us will naturally affect our behavior, and others will notice. First John 2:3–6 says, "We know that we have come to know him if we obey his commands. The man who says, 'I know him,' but does not do what he commands is a liar, and the truth is not in him. But if anyone obeys his word, God's love is truly made complete in him. This is how we know we are in him: Whoever claims to be in him must walk as Jesus did."

Has your life been changed by trusting in Christ as your Savior? You can make the decision now to trust Jesus and be saved. You can be known by others as one who loves God. Let's pray.

COOKS AND CREATION

Set and Props—Seating is in an arena layout, with three tables at the head of the room. Each table is covered with protective covering and a variety of bowls, spatulas, and other bakeware, as well as containers of flour, milk, and eggs. Include a decorated cake on a plate. A picture of a cathedral and a classical music CD to play to the students are also needed. Design a sign to hang overhead that reads "Baker's Bonanza." A curtain on a rod is optional and may be used to cover the set until characters take their places.

Characters, each wearing their unique apron and humorous chef hat.
—Ben Bang
—Eva Lution
—Daniel Design
—Host
—Teacher

The lights are off. Students enter the room and take seats. Play talking Bible or have a reader read Genesis 1–2:2:

> In the beginning God created the heavens and the earth. Now the earth was formless and empty, darkness was over the surface of the deep, and the spirit of God was hovering over the waters. And God said, "Let there be light," and

there was light. God saw that the light was good, and he separated the light from darkness. God called the light "day" and the darkness he called "night." And there was evening, and there was morning-the first day. And God said, "Let there be an expanse between the waters to separate water from water." So God made the expanse and separated the water under the expanse from the water above it. And it was so. God called the expanse "sky." And there was evening and there was morning—the second day. And God said, "Let the water under the sky be gathered to one place, and let the dry ground appear." And it was so. God called the dry ground "'land," and the gathered waters he called "seas." And God saw that it was good.

Then God said "Let the land produce vegetation: seed-bearing plants and trees on the land that bear fruit with seed in it, according to their various kinds." And it was so. The land produced vegetation: plants bearing seed according to their kinds and trees bearing fruit with seed in it according to their kinds. And God saw that it as good. And there was evening and there was morning—the third day. And God said, "Let there be lights in the expanse of the sky to separate the day from the night, and let them serve as signs to mark seasons and days and years, and let them be lights in the expanse of the sky to give light on the earth." And it was so. God made two great lights—the greater light to govern the day and the lesser light to govern the night. He also made the stars. God set them in the expanse of the sky to give light on the earth, to govern the day and the night, and to separate light form darkness. And God saw that it was good. And there was evening, and there was morning - the fourth day. And God saw that it was good. God blessed them and said, "Be fruitful and increase in number and fill the water in the seas, and let the birds increase on the earth." And there was evening and there was morning—the fifth day . And God said, "Let the land produce living creatures according to their kinds: livestock, creatures that move on the ground, and wild animals each according to its kind." And it was so. God made the wild animals each according to its kind. And it was so. God made the wild animals according to their kinds, the livestock according to their kinds, and all the creatures that move along the ground according to their kinds. And God saw that it was good.

Then God said, "Let us make man in our image, in our likeness, and let them rule over the fish of the sea and the birds of the air, over the livestock, over all the earth, and over all the creatures that move along the ground." So God created man in his own image, in the image of god he created him; male and female he created them. God blessed them and said to them, "be fruitful and increase in number; fill the earth and subdue it. Rule over the fish of the sea and the birds of the air and every living creature that moves on the ground." And God said, "I give you every seed-bearing plant on the face of the earth and every tree that has fruit with seed in it. They will be yours for food. And to all the beasts of the earth and all the birds of the air and all the creatures that move on the ground—everything that has the breath of life in it—I give every green plant for food." And it was so. God saw all that he had made and it was very good. And there was evening, and there was morning—the sixth day.

Thus was the heavens and the earth were completed in all their vast array. By the seventh day God had finished his work he had been doing; so on the seventh day he rested from all his work.

(*Turn on lights.*)

Three chefs enter and stand at their respective stations. As the students enter, chefs greet them and show off their cooking tools.

(*Open curtain if used.*)

HOST. (*The host stands near tables.*) Welcome to Baker's Bonanza! Today we will view each of our featured chef's techniques in baking a scrumptious dessert. We will see how each approaches the task of creating the winning entry. To all—good luck!

(*All chefs take a bow when introduced.*)

In kitchen #1, we have Ben Bang, who makes an art of producing pastry using his unique method of throwing things together. Of course, we never know what surprise we will have when he takes his masterpiece out of the oven.

(*Ben Bang throws flour, eggs, and other ingredients into a bowl and mixes things up. This will and should make a little mess, as this should be done with much flair, so place plastic on the floor to catch the mess.*)

HOST. Next we have, in kitchen #2, our very own Eva Lution. Her strict theories of creating confections cause us to realize what patience is all about. We will see just how her theories work in reality.

(*Eva Lution places the ingredients around the bowl. She then just sits and stares at it.*)

HOST. Last but not least, I introduce to you, in kitchen #3, the most unpopular of chefs, Daniel Design. Mr. Design has the novel belief that a chef should actually follow a plan for his confection. Can you imagine that? Planning the creation of a cake! Oh well, to each his own. As each chef waits for their masterpiece to be done, we will discuss the various ways used to create the perfect dessert.

TEACHER. Much like we illustrate with our chefs and their finished product, let us talk about how people view the creation of the place we live—the earth and our universe. As you have read in Genesis, in God's Word, we know God has created each aspect of our universe and all that is on earth, including ourselves. God created different things on different days, and the final day of the week was used for rest. Hebrews 11:3 says, "By faith we understand that the universe was formed at God's command, so that what is seen was not made out of what was visible." Also, we read in Isaiah 40:26, "Lift your eyes and look to the heavens: Who created all these? He who brings out the starry host one by one, and calls them each by name. Because of his great power and mighty strength, not one of them is missing."

Man has tried to explain God's creation by other means and calling it scientific reasoning. One explanation is represented by chef #1—dumping everything together and hoping everything comes out to perfection. This might be like the big bang theory. This theory basically states that after a large collision or explosion, matter, molecules, and substances combined in a certain way and with enough time, produced life. This line of thought leads us to believe that all happened by the right conditions and random chance, not by a plan or a design. Just like you need to know what ingredients, what order, and at what temperature and time to bake a good cake, do you not think an intelligent design was needed to create our universe, earth, and the life that inhabits it?

Let's see. (*Shows a picture of cathedral.*) Could this have been created by the big bang theory? Can materials just thrown together and by some random chance end up with this architectural jewel? Or how about this? (*Play part of a classical music piece.*) Just a bunch of random notes that happened to fall into the correct sequence? Hardly possible, in fact, impossible without the creator and designer, God. We can rejoice in what God has given us as we read Psalm 19:1: "The heavens declare the glory of God; the skies proclaim the work of his hands."

Now, the next man-made theory is a very popular one, evolution. I think many of you have heard about this on television or in school. Our chef who is creating a cake by letting the ingredients do their own combining and baking is somewhat like this theory. Do you think these ingredients will surely come together and transform into a cake? Evolution is based on the idea that a progressive change takes place—or the development of an organ or species takes place—changing into one that is more complex than the original. This is why they say man has evolved from a lower form of man, and this one from a lower form, and that one from an even lower form, back to man's evolution from apes. This is taken even further by saying that apes were evolved from simple creatures and even single-celled organisms. Of course, all of this is said to take a long time.

Does this actually sound possible? Is there anything you can think of that generates or becomes something better or more complex than it was before all by itself? "Entropy" is the scientific term for the natural breaking down of things over the course of time. Things naturally decompose, rust, fall apart, and wear out. Have you ever seen a house look better and better without any maintenance? No, the house would deteriorate.

Our chef Eva Lution is very patient, but I doubt that without her doing anything to get her cake mixed up and baked that it will be a success.

Our third contestant is Daniel Design, and he has measured his ingredients, mixed the batter properly, and poured the batter into cake pans to bake. Daniel has set the oven at a certain temperature and will bake his cake for the right length of time. Mr. Design believes in a plan and knows that through this thought and care he will have a good cake. Isaiah 42:5–6 says, "This is what God the Lord says—he who created the heavens and stretched them out, who spread out the earth and all that comes out of it, who gives breath to his people, and life to those who walk on it: I, the Lord, have called you in righteousness; I will take hold of your hand.

I will keep you and will make you to be a covenant for the people and a light for the Gentiles."

Today we have only scratched the surface in explaining why we believe what the Bible says about God's creation in Genesis. More importantly, we want to share with you that God not only created us but has a reason for creating each of us, and that is to have fellowship with us. God loves us very much and has a plan for us to know him.

Sin has separated us from God, who is completely holy. Romans 3:23 says, "For all have sinned and fall short of the glory of God." God has given us the gift of life and the gift of a spiritual life through his son, Jesus. Romans 6:23 says, "For the wages of sin is death, but the gift of God is eternal life in Jesus Christ our Lord."

What decision will you make today to know God? It says in Romans 10:9, "That if you confess with your mouth, 'Jesus is Lord,' and believe in your heart that God raised him from the dead, you will be saved."

(*Lead students in prayer.*)

HOST. Okay everybody, let's take a look at the finished cakes our chefs have worked so hard on. Ben Bang, please show us how your idea for a cake worked. (*Shrugging, Ben shows the bowl of mixed-up ingredients.*) Oh well, I guess that big bang theory didn't work out so well. I'm sorry, Ben.

Now let's take a look at Eva's creative solution for our Baker's Bonanza! Eva, Eva, *Eva!* Wake up! (*The host shakes her.*) You have waited for such a long time for all this stuff to come together and make something delicious. Take a look. Does this look like a cake? Sorry, Eva. Maybe we need about another ten thousand more years. (*Eva goes back to sleep.*)

Well, we have one contestant left; it's Daniel Design. Mr. Design, please take your cake out and show us if following a plan has given you a great result. (*Daniel shows a beautifully decorated cake.*) All right, Daniel is the winner and has done a great job. Give him a hand. (*Everyone claps.*)

Ready for some cake everyone? (*Serves cake to class.*)

DOORS TO NOWHERE—DOOR TO SOMEWHERE

Props—Heavy-looking wooden door; cardboard made to look like car door with window cut out; cardboard box painted white with trap door cut into top; jail door made of dowels on a frame; screen door, and a lightweight, wooden, plain paneled door.

Characters—One for each door dressed as follows.

> Heavy wooden door, dressed in jeans, work shirt, and boots.
> Car door, dressed in jacket and tie or nicely dressed.
> Trap door, dressed in black pants or dark jeans and dark top.
> Jail door, dressed in black and white or bright orange jailhouse garb.
> Screen door, dressed in flowing lightweight clothes and scarf in pastel colors.
> Plain paneled door, dressed in khakis and shirt or jeans and shirt.
> Narrator

NARRATOR. Have you ever considered what doors do for us and what different types of doors tell us? Doors are the entrances or exits to somewhere or something. They are designed to perform some kind of function.

Doors may also tell us something about their owner. Take the front door of your house, for example. We could have a front door that is very fancy or painted a color that looks beautiful from the street. (*May show pictures of the following.*) Imagine the different feelings we might have seeing a formal, black front door with bright brass door knockers, kickplates, and hardware. How about walking up to a house with a bright yellow door? Some people have red, beige, or even wooden-stained doors. Each gives you a different impression. Now if we think about the basement door, we may think of something more rundown or plain, maybe plain wood or metal, nothing that special. Yet it's necessary to get in and out of the basement and needs to be durable.

Have you ever thought about doors as being portals or transitions to somewhere or something else? We often talk about opportunities being "open" or "closed" doors and believe this will help with our decision making and the future. For instance, when I was applying to different colleges and then to get a job, I prayed to God to guide my decisions. I assumed a rejection was a closed door and an acceptance as an open door. Of course, when I was accepted at more than one place, I prayed for further direction and had to make decisions based on other things. Sometimes we must choose the right door based on what God tells us in Scripture.

(Screen door enters, dancing around and holding the door.)

We may have the screen door, for instance.

SCREEN DOOR. I just don't know what to think. Marjie tells me one thing, and Katrina tells me another. How do I decide? Maybe it's about karma, feng shui, or something like that. I'm a peace lover and open to everything. I just can't make a decision, but I'll find the answer blowing in the wind!

NARRATOR. A Scripture that talks of this kind of decision making is James 1:6–8: "But when he asks, he must believe and not doubt, because he who doubts is like the wave of the sea, blown and tossed by the wind, that man should not think he will receive anything from the Lord; he is a double-minded man, unstable in all he does." A screen door allows the breeze inside but is the wrong kind of door to provide security or to pattern our lives after.

(Heavy wooden door stomps in, plunks down door, and stands with hands on hips.)

HEAVY WOODEN DOOR. There now, that shouldn't go anywhere! Let's see 'em try to break into this door and take my stuff! I want everybody who sees this door know they will go no further without my permission. I'm not a pushover and don't bend in the breeze. (Looks at screen door.) Nobody tells me what to do. I make up my own mind, you hear me? (Points at the audience.)

NARRATOR. Going up to this door might make you just a little bit nervous, don't you think? First Samuel 15:23 says, "For rebellion is as bad as witchcraft and stubbornness is as sin and idolatry, because thou has rejected the Word of the Lord." Pride and stubbornness are attitudes the Lord does not honor, so we should be careful not to go through this type of door . Now let's see if there are any other types of doors we have not seen yet. Oh, here comes one!

(Trap door enters cautiously, opens top, and peeks out.)

TRAP DOOR. Well hello. I'm glad to see everyone. (Trap Door top suddenly shuts.)

NARRATOR. Oh, come on now. We won't bite! Just look at all the people here to meet you.

(*Trap door opens slightly and looks out.*)

NARRATOR. Let me introduce you to our group.

(*Trap door shuts again.*)

NARRATOR. It's fine. You don't have to shut that door. Don't be afraid. (*Turns to speak to the audience.*) I guess our trap door is a little afraid or shy of everyone. How about encouraging it to open up a little bit. (*Allow audience response.*)

(*Trap door opens cautiously, looks out, and steps to side.*)

NARRATOR. Let me share a verse with you. It's Joshua 1:9: "Be strong and very courageous. Do not be terrified; do not be discouraged for the Lord your God will be with you wherever you go." Now, trap door, does this Scripture help you?

(*Trap door nods.*)

NARRATOR. Let's give trap door a hand for being courageous! (*Allow audience response.*)

(*Trap door smiles and stands behind other doors.*)

NARRATOR. We have seen so many kinds of doors. I don't know if I can think of any others. Can you?

(*Car door enters deliberately and proudly.*)

NARRATOR. How do you do. (*Reaches out hand to shake it.*)

(*Car door does not respond to handshake.*)

NARRATOR. Isn't this group great? What do think of all these kids?

(*Car door sniffs and looks away.*)

CAR DOOR. I suppose they are all right. Just so they don't mess up my door. You know I paid a lot of money for this fine door.

NARRATOR. I'm sure they will respect your beautiful door. I can really appreciate how nice it is.

CAR DOOR. Well, I don't know if you can. After all, only those with taste and class could own one of these—and in this beautiful custom finish. (*Rubs hand over door.*) My parents always told me I deserved the best. I better step aside now. I wouldn't want anyone to mar my finish.

NARRATOR. In chapter 11 of Proverbs we can read, "When pride comes, then comes disgrace; but with humility comes wisdom." If our attitude reflects pride, others will not like us, and God will not, either. God blesses a humble attitude.

(*Jail door enters and looks out from behind the bars.*)

JAIL DOOR. Hey, you over there. You got the key to this door?

NARRATOR. No I don't, but even if I did, I don't think they would want me to let you out.

JAIL DOOR. I'll tell you like I told the others—*I didn't do it.* I was framed. You can't trust anybody these days. You know what I mean?

NARRATOR. It looks to me like you chose the wrong door and went down the wrong path.

JAIL DOOR. I told you they framed me. I was at the wrong place at the wrong time. Just because I was in the clink before does not mean I'm a repeat offender. And even if I was, a guy has to look out for himself.

(*Looks out at the audience.*) Hey, any of you guys have the key to this thing? It stinks in here.

NARRATOR. Galatians 3:22 says, "But the scripture declares that the whole world is a prisoner of sin, so that what was promised, being given through faith in Jesus Christ, might be given to those that believe." As it says in this verse, we are all born into sin and need to pass through the prison door to the freedom Christ gives. The key to that door is belief in what Jesus did for us on the cross. Have you confessed your sin and asked Jesus to forgive you? Romans 3:23 says, "For all have sinned and come short of the glory of God."

(*Jail door stands to the side.*)

NARRATOR. Well, it looks like we have another door coming to visit us. This one looks like an ordinary door, not fancy or heavy or having some special meaning. I wonder what is behind it. (*Knocks on door.*)

(*Door opens and hands Bible to narrator.*)

NARRATOR. A Bible. Let's see what is bookmarked in it. (*Shows a heart-shaped card.*) Revelation 3:19: "So be earnest and repent. Here I am! I stand at the door and knock. If anyone hears my voice and opens the door, I will come in and eat with him, and he with me." Each of us has the opportunity to let the truth of God's Word touch our heart and mind. Will you make the life-changing decision to answer the knock on your heart's door? Will you believe God's Word and believe Jesus came to save you for your sins? Will you open the door of your heart as Jesus knocks on it? You have the opportunity today to make this important choice in your life. You will be walking through a new door in your life and will change through the power of God.

(*Conclude with a prayer.*)

DUCT TAPE HEALING

Set and Props—Surgical suite setting, with a table with white sheets (bottom and top). Knives and instruments are on one side, neatly laid out. On the other side of the table are a roll of duct tape and scissors. If available, place any hospital props nearby, such as an IV drip, heart monitor, and stethoscopes.

Characters—Patient with two broken arms.
    Surgeon in scrubs, mask, cap, and gloves.
    Surgical assistant in scrubs, mask, cap, and gloves.
    Surgeon in scrubs and a cap made of paper and duct tape.
    Surgical assistant in scrubs with a duct tape cap.

(*Duct tape surgeon and assistant enter, carrying patient in great pain. The patient is moaning and groaning loudly, creating much confusion.*)

DUCT TAPE SURGEON. Hurry up! Let's get this guy on the table. He's in really bad shape.

DUCT TAPE SURGICAL ASSISTANT. Lighten up, Doc. I can't go but so fast. I think I ate too much pizza for lunch.

DUCT TAPE SURGEON. Okay, let's get him up on the table. Ready? One, two, three—uuup. (*Roughly lifts patient onto the table.*)

DUCT TAPE SURGICAL ASSISTANT. Now what are we going to do to patch this guy up, Doc? (*Reaches for the duct tape, unrolling some and cutting it off.*)

DUCT TAPE SURGEON. (*Wipes forehead.*) I don't know. Let me think for a minute. Man, I wish I had a soda right now.

DUCT TAPE SURGICAL ASSISTANT. Hey, do you want me to get a couple of sodas real quick, Doc?

DUCT TAPE SURGEON. What is wrong with you? Do you have a brain or not? We can't just go trotting off and leave this guy here. We need to figure out how to fix his arms.

(*Patient sighs and falls asleep.*)

(*Surgeon and surgical assistant enter, quickly look over the patient, and whisper to each other about treatment.*)

SURGEON. We need to get started with surgery, and you folks need to calm down so we can work on both arms before infection and fever set in.

SURGICAL ASSISTANT. Okay, we are scrubbed in. Let's get started on the right arm.

(*Surgeon and assistant take their place and quietly start surgery, speaking softly to each other. Assistant hands various instruments to the surgeon, who works behind the sheet on one arm.*)

DUCT TAPE SURGEON. Okay, hand me that scissors. No, no, no, I mean the scalpel. Uh, why don't you help me?

DUCT TAPE SURGICAL ASSISTANT. You are the surgeon. You tell me what you need.

DUCT TAPE SURGEON. I know! Let's take a peek over there at them. (*Points to other surgical team.*) Hey, what are you guys doing? Oh, I see. Maybe we can set the arm first.

DUCT TAPE SURGICAL ASSISTANT. How are you going to do that?

DUCT TAPE SURGEON. Get ready. Let's yank!

(*Patient moans loudly.*)

SURGEON. No! Don't do that. You will hurt the patient.

DUCT TAPE SURGEON. Okay assistant, hand me that duct tape now!

(*Duct tape assistant hands surgeon duct tape, who unrolls the duct tape and starts winding it around the patient's arm.*)

DUCT TAPE SURGEON. Now this is more like it. We might be able to fix this arm with duct tape, because you know they say anything can be fixed with duct tape.

SURGEON. Let's go ahead and finish this up. He will be as good as new in a week or so. We will schedule a follow-up appointment to remove his cast and see that the arm is healed properly.

(*Patient wakes up.*)

SURGICAL ASSISTANT. (*Speaks to patient.*) How are you feeling? (*Patient nods.*) We have your arm fixed now, and it should mend nicely in the next few weeks.

SURGEON. You will have some discomfort for a few days, but we will schedule therapy. Right now you just take it easy and get some rest. I'll stop by your room later.

(*Surgeon and assistant leave the room.*)

DUCT TAPE SURGEON. Man, I'm starving. I think this guy will make it all right. (*Turns to duct tape surgical assistant.*) What do you think?

DUCT TAPE SURGICAL ASSISTANT. Hey, how about Burger King. Oh, yes, this guy will be fine. Let's get going.

DUCT TAPE SURGEON. (*Turns to patient.*) Hey dude, you doing good? You know we did our best, but as they say, no pain no gain. Know what I mean?

(*Patient, surgeon, and surgical assistant nod their heads as they leave.*)

(*Patient stays; duct tape surgeon and assistant leave.*)

DUCT TAPE SURGEON. Hey, I'm hungry. Let's go!

DUCT TAPE SURGICAL ASSISTANT. Yeah, this guy is gonna be just fine. You know what they say—duct tape fixes everything.

DUCT TAPE SURGEON. We are the duct tape kings! (*Surgeon and assistant give each other high fives.*)

(*Patient sits up and speaks to audience.*)

PATIENT. Which arm do you folks think will heal properly? (*Allow response.*)

That is right, the one treated by the real doctor, who knew what he was doing. You know, this skit shows us there are real doctors and fake ones. Fake healing, like what we saw with the duct tape surgeon and his assistant, will not produce the correct results and will end in tragedy. Our spiritual lives, our hearts also need healing, because the Bible tells us in Romans 3:23 that we are all sinners: "For all have sinned and come short of the glory of God." People will often try anything to fill a need they feel inside. That emptiness or need is a sinful nature, and they need to reach out to God and be healed. Our sin has separated us from God, and he provides a way to get rid of the sin through the forgiveness of Jesus, God's only son. Psalm 103:1–5 says, "Praise the Lord, O my soul, all my inmost being, praise his holy name. Praise the Lord and forget not all his benefits. He forgives all my sins and heals all my diseases; he redeems my life from the pit and crowns me with love and compassion. He satisfies my desires with good things, so that my youth is renewed like the eagle's."

Jesus came into this world to be a perfect example for us, to heal people, to give his life, and to rise from the dead to forgive our sins. Our eternal spirit is healed and our sins forgiven by the great gift Jesus has given us—if we believe and accept him into our lives. Isaiah 53:5 says, "But he was pierced for our transgressions, he was crushed for our iniquities; the punishment that brought us peace was upon him, and by his stripes we are healed."

Will you accept the gift of Jesus God has given you and trust him with your life? Or will you settle for a duct tape patch up? Do not try one more fake thing in this world to fill your inner need. Trust Christ Jesus today, and let him save you.

(Conclude with prayer or commitment.)

GRAVY AS SIN

Characters –Teacher.

Mushroom gravy—Wear brown and white or tan colors, pad with lumps under clothes. Use makeup to create brown and white spots on face, hands, etc. To simulate the underside of the mushroom (the gills), use an eyeliner to draw parallel lines close together on palms, around eyes, or anywhere skin is exposed. You may also paint your tongue.

Redeye gravy—Wear dark colors with alternating padded and unpadded areas under clothes. Using food coloring, suckers, or another means, color tongue blue or black. Using makeup, make circles under the eyes with red, purple, and black to make the eyes look sunken in.

Giblet gravy—Dress in tan and brown colors. Put stuffing under clothes to create lumps all over body. Wear a stuffed, knit skullcap to create lumps. Chew wads of gum and stuff in both cheeks.

Tomato gravy—Dress in oranges and reds. Put pillows under clothes around the middle. Wear a red or orange hat. Paint red circular spots on all exposed skin.

(As each gravy character enters, teacher steps back and the next gravy character enters. After all gravy characters have said their parts, they will step back and let the teacher come forward to continue the lesson.)

TEACHER. Welcome to our class. Our panel of guests will discuss with you the benefits—as they see it—of this wonderful fountain of youth, or the fountain of gravy. Do you enjoy eating gravy with your meals? (*Allow response.*) Good for you! These guests are just a sampling of many people around us who have taken gravy eating to new heights. They will share with us something about themselves, so listen closely.

MUSHROOM GRAVY. I've always been a meat-and-potatoes kind of a (*Use guy or gal, whichever is appropriate.*) but never thought much about gravy. One day my friend told me to try a little bit. He said it would taste sooo good going down. I tried it, but I didn't like it that much. It was just that … like … all of my friends kept eating gravy all the time, mostly on their potatoes, but on a bunch of other stuff, too.

My friend told me that maybe I needed to try a different kind of gravy. You know, like different strokes for different folks. So I tried a few kinds. But when I tried mushroom gravy, I kinda liked it. *Maybe just in small amounts,* I thought. Well the more I hung out with my friends, the more I had a taste for the mushroom gravy. After a few months, I used more and more of it, and not just on potatoes. Yes, I used it on carrots and beans and beef and fish. I used more and more of it. My friends just thought it was the coolest thing that I loved mushroom gravy so much. They told me just to ignore the funny lines that started showing up on my body and the spots, too. No, these things didn't really matter, because everybody has problems. Right? What's a few spots gonna hurt? It doesn't bother me. I just stay close to the cool guys. Yea, my gravy eaters; we have a blast together!

REDEYE GRAVY. I've always had problems with my mom. We argue a lot. But I know she has a hard time, especially after the divorce. I am my own person, though, and need to express myself and do my own thing. My mom warned me that I might end up like her—slopping all this gravy over hash browns, biscuits, and even country ham. Well I don't want to be like her, a loser on a dead-end street. But as I get older, it just seems like I can't help but become more and more like her. Scary, huh?

I married this guy who had to have redeye gravy with his meals—every meal. He would dump the stuff on everything, even his chocolate cake for dessert! We argued and fought. I knew I was better than that. I couldn't stand it. There I was, living with this louse, just like my mother had done. Even though I didn't know my dad, Mom said he made life miserable with his sloshing all that redeye gravy on everything.

Maybe it's in my genes or maybe just habit, but I gave up fighting. I just started eating the redeye gravy along with my husband. He was proud of me and said he hoped we had a whole bunch of children—little ones running around with gravy-smeared cheeks. My life is not what I wanted, but I'm okay. Redeye gravy does make me feel better some days. Who knows what life is supposed to be about anyway. The gravy does take the edge off. This is as good as it gets, I guess. Oh, it's time for me to fix supper. Biscuits and redeye gravy tonight.

GIBLET GRAVY. I've always been brought up to eat my food and not drink it. My parents told me to beware of those giblets in the turkey. What are giblets anyway? My father told me the giblets get a foothold, and you just can't stop eating them. My mother always taught me that drowning good food with gravy is wrong. I obeyed my parents and knew they told me these things for my own good. They wanted to spare me the pain of eating gravy and the life that goes along with it.

When I got out of the house and went to college, away from my parent's watchful eyes, I noticed lots of popular kids would put this giblet gravy on their dinner, and it didn't do them any harm. My parents are pretty old-fashioned anyway. Maybe they are just superstitious or something. I even thought that since they served so much of it at school, it had to be all right, maybe even make you smarter! That was the beginning of the road of my eating giblet gravy. I just ate a little at a time, but it seemed as time went by, my stomach could hold more and more. The guys on the soccer team used to say, "Boy, you can sure hold your gravy!" I would tilt my plate up to drink it, and suddenly, a giblet would fall into my throat. Man, I would almost gag! Once I did choke on a gizzard. Fortunately, they got it out of my throat at the school clinic, because I really didn't want my parents to know. I'm not such a bad person, gravy has not really affected me.

TOMATO GRAVY. My mama always taught me to behave like a lady and be the best I could be. Yes, I am a good person and was always a good girl. My daddy said I was his little princess, and nothing was too good for me. My family wasn't like those poor people who live over in the poor section of town. No, we lived properly, went to all the right schools, and went to church every Sunday. My mama always bought me the prettiest dresses to wear to God's house—to be an example, you know. Oh, one time I was just mortified. The laundry lady forgot about a gravy stain on my beautiful, cream, silk dress. Right up front! My mama said she would scold that laundry woman. Why no daughter of hers was going to God's house with a stain on her dress. Yes, we were better than that! We are not like those horrible gravy eaters on the other side of town.

My mama taught me that we must sip our gravy, not gulp it down like the men do. My daddy is so funny; he tries to be a gentleman but sometimes gets carried away eating the tomato gravy. Now I like my tomato gravy, too, but I am certainly a lady about it. My mama says that only the better people eat tomato gravy. (*Sniff.*) Our family is cultured and sophisticated; it is our lot in life, you know. Sometimes it is such a burden to be an example to the uncouth. (Looks from side to side.) I've always eaten my tomato gravy properly, just as my mama and her mama before her did. Not to do so would be a sin. I admit the taste of that gravy over my asparagus almost gets the better of me, but I always mind my manners and do what is right.

Of course, after all these years of eating tomato gravy, my family has a little complexion problem. But that's all right, because my mama taught me how to fix myself up just right. We do all we can to hide the negative effects of tomato gravy, but only because it has so many benefits. I know when I have children and teach them how to be responsible gravy eaters, and the image our family has to uphold, I will be so blessed. Such is the burden I bear.

TEACHER. Proverbs 14: 9 says, "Fools mock sin, but the godly acknowledge it and seek forgiveness." If gravy in these people's lives is like sin, wouldn't you think they would see the harm it has on their bodies and attitudes? Don't you think they would stop eating gravy and stop making excuses? Many times in our lives sin is like the gravy in the lives of these people—attitudes and actions that get hold of you and mold you into folks who do not please Jesus. The way to break these wrong attitudes and actions is to admit sin is wrong and be sorry for your sin. I will read Romans 3:23: "For all have sinned and fall short of the glory of God." We are all sinners and need to admit this and seek forgiveness.

Next we need to understand God provided a way out of the sin and to receive forgiveness through the gift of Jesus. Jesus came to take sin, and he died on the cross and rose from the dead to overcome its power and provide us with forgiveness and new life. Let us read Romans 6:23: "For the wages of sin is death, but the gift of God is eternal life in Jesus Christ our Lord." When we believe we are sinners and what Jesus has done for us and then seek forgiveness for our sins and trust him as our Savior, we become new people. Our old life is transformed into a new one, as we read in 2 Corinthians 5:17: "Therefore, if anyone is in Christ, he is a new creation; the old has gone, the new has come!" Will you be like these who are so caught up in their own gravy as sin, or will you take a stand today and choose a new life?

(Ask for decisions and pray.)

KNOW YOUR H$_2$O

Props —Either a handheld water bottle with a face painted on it or a costume that replicates a water bottle.
Small bottles of water for each person to hand out at end.

Character—Facilitator

FACILITATOR. Hello! I hope all of you are doing well today. I would like to tell you a little about myself. After all, without me you would not be alive right now! My chemical composition is H$_2$O, but you can just call me water.

If you try to think of all the ways I am used, the list is endless. For instance, I get spread pretty thin when I am rubbed on windows, and it sometimes scares me when I am hauled up the side of a tall building. After the window cleaners rub me onto the windows, they take a rubber squeegee and wipe me off. That hurts! Sometimes I am mixed with some strong, smelly chemicals and sloshed around on the floor with a mop. Yes, I clean the floor and disinfect it with those chemicals, but it often gives me a bad headache. Now let's see. Oh, here is something I get involved in that is a lot of fun. Have you ever heard of whitewater? Well in my natural state, I gather with many streams of water and go rushing downhill over rocks and under trees to form a river. Sometimes people will get in rafts and try to maneuver around my rapids. It is so funny to see this. People often fly out of those rafts because the ride is so wild.

While I just told you about some fun times, I will now tell you about a very important job I do for every one of you. This job is smelly and nasty, but it's important. I help flush away waste and keep your kitchen and bathroom germ-free. The officials call me "waste water" when I do this. It may not be pretty but somebody has to do it, right?

I haven't talked about how much flexibility I have. I can change my form depending on what temperature I am. For example, I become a solid when frozen and can be used to cool your drinks with ice cubes. I can also be used to skate on. Sometimes, depending on weather conditions, I form into frozen flakes that fall from the sky. This can be good or bad. When these frozen flakes pile up, it is very hard for people to drive to work or school. It is, however, much fun for sledding, skiing, or even having a good snowball fight.

When I am put into a pot on the stove and heat is applied, my temperature increases, and I can cook your food. When I am heated, I will make your back feel so good when I run down it in the shower. I know I may not have an exciting flavor on my own, but lots of you add flavoring to me and like the taste. I can be flavored with tea, fruit, or even chocolate powder with marshmallows added.

An interesting thing about me is that when I am boiled, my form changes from liquid to steam or water vapor. Sometimes steam is used to help people with a head cold, and other times, steam can be used to create electricity by turning large turbines.

I know God has created me for a purpose, but sometimes I feel people take me for granted and waste me. I help people in many ways and am necessary for life. In fact, a large percentage of your body is made up me. You cannot survive long without me. If people, animals, or plants do not have enough of me each day, they will die.

Did you know the Bible even talks about the importance of water? Let me read you what happened in John 4.

> Now Jesus had to go through Samaria. So he came to a town in Samaria called Sychar; ... Jacob's well was there. And Jesus, tired as he was from the journey, sat down by the well. It was about noon time. When a Samaritan woman came to draw water, Jesus said to her, "Will you give me a drink?" The Samaritan woman said to him, "You are a Jew and I am a Samaritan woman. How can you ask me for a drink?" (For Jews do not associate with Samaritans.) Jesus answered her, "If you knew the gift of God and who it is that asks you for a drink, you would have asked him and he would have giving you living water." "Sir," the woman said, "you have nothing to draw with and the well is deep. Where can you get this living water? Are you greater than our father Jacob, who gave us this well and drank from it himself, as did his sons and flocks and herds?" Jesus answered, "Everyone who drinks the water will be thirsty again, but whoever drinks the water I give him will never thirst. Indeed the water I give him will become in him a spring of water welling up to eternal life." The woman said to him, "Sir, give me this water so I won't get thirty and have to keep coming here to draw water."

The conversation continued, and we see the woman did not understand about the "living water" Jesus was talking about. This woman thought Jesus was talking about the religious beliefs of her forefathers, not the life change Jesus provides to those who place their trust in Him. While well water can be used to clean dirty things, the living water Jesus talks about cleanses us from our sins. In Romans 3:23 it says, "For all have sinned and come short of the glory of God," and Isaiah 1:18 says, "Though your sins are like scarlet, they shall be white as snow; though they are as red as crimson, they shall be like wool." Well water hydrates our bodies and energizes us, while the living water of Jesus energizes our spirit and gives us a new life in him.

Do you believe Jesus is the only way to salvation from our sins? Will you confess you are a sinner and seek forgiveness through the gift of Jesus' death on the cross? Will you rejoice in knowing you are free to leave your old life behind and have a new life because Jesus rose from the grave? You can have your spiritual thirst quenched and have the promise of eternal life in heaven if you accept this life-giving water and trust in Jesus with your whole heart and mind.

(*Invite the audience to trust in Jesus and pray.*)

(*Pass out bottles of water to everyone.*)

LUMPS OF CLAY

Set and Props—Table with plastic cover, decorative and functional items made of pottery, block of modeling clay, and bowl of water.
Facilitator
How many of you have ever worked with clay like this? (*Show a piece of clay. Show various items made of clay and explain what they are used for.*)

Things made of clay take on various forms. Some are for practical use, like cooking or flowerpots, and some are for beauty or decorative use. These items are similar to people. We are created with blood, bones, and skin, and we have many other likenesses as God created us. However, we are all different in personality and in our strengths, weaknesses, and abilities. And we also look different.

(*Take a lump of clay and begin to soften it. Demonstrate each technique.*)

Different techniques can be used to turn a piece of clay into something. One way to make things is the coil method. This method is best suited for making pots or containers. Watch as I show you. You take a small piece of clay and roll it between your palms or on a flat surface, forming a snake or coil. Make more of these and stack them to create what you want. After you have the basic shape you want, wet your fingers with water and smooth out the object. Add any details you want.

Another technique of working with clay is to mold it by pressing it in your hands and fingers to create the shape and form you like. After creating the form, wet your fingers and smooth it out. Finish it in the way you like. A potter can use a mechanized potter's wheel to spin a lump of clay. You wet your hands and run them over the clay to make it into a pot or other form you want.

Finishing the surfaces of these creations can be done using various tools. Texture can be added to the surface of soft clay by pressing something into the clay, thus leaving its pattern. Premade molds may be used to press designs into the soft clay, and any sharp or pointed item can be used to make any texture you want. It is limited only by your imagination.

We have discussed what a potter does, but what is a person called who works with clay, stone, wood, or other material to create a decorative or functional object? This person is called a sculptor and uses special tools to form different materials.

Getting back to the clay pottery, we know most items are finished by hardening after color is added. A special paint, called a glaze, is applied where you want it. The glaze looks very dull and flat when you apply it to the clay, but when you place the item into an oven or kiln and heat it to a very high temperature, the item becomes brilliant and shiny. Various things such as salt can be placed into the kiln when fired, and these things change the chemical makeup of the glaze, giving it interesting and different effects.

Each piece of pottery or sculpture is unique, much like us. God also made us unique, as told in Isaiah 64:8: "Yet, O Lord, you are our father. We are the clay and you are the potter. We are all the work of your hand."

God created you and I in his image, and he has a special purpose for us. You may think you are not good-looking, not as smart as you would like to be, or not very talented. But do you know what? God does not make mistakes, and he knows you. God loves you and sent Jesus, his only Son, to earth to take our sins to the cross, where he died. Three days later, he rose from the grave to prove he is God and has victory over our sins and death. If you believe what the Bible tells us about Jesus and confess your sins, he will save us and give us a new purpose for our life. In Jesus we can find fulfillment and joy in our lives.

We all have hard times, but some of you may think you are just a messed-up person and should have never been born. This type of thinking is a trick from Satan, who only wants to destroy you. We need to read what is written in Romans 9:19, 20: "Who resists God's will, but who are you O man to talk back to God? Shall what is formed say to him who formed it, why did you make me like this? Does not the potter have the right to make out of the same lump of clay some pottery for noble purposes and some for common use?" Let us study God's Word to grow, and let us realize God made us like we are to fulfill his purposes for us in this life.

If you are struggling with issues about yourself and these verses spoke to you in a special way, we pray and ask the Lord to make a change in your attitude and heart. We pray you will be aware of the special gifts and abilities you have and that the Lord will give you the determination to work on them and improve yourself.

(*Say a prayer.*)

MINE

Set and Props—Card table with four chairs. Brightly colored and patterned tablecloth; four paper plates filled with potato chips; four 3 × 5 cards, each a different color, numbered one through four; and four stacks of dominoes (about five to six per stack). Also, a poster with following printed: Envy—A feeling of discontent or ill-will because of another's advantage or possessions; resentful dislike of another who has something that one desires. Another poster with the following printed: Greed—Wanting or taking all that you can get, with no thought of others' need.

Characters—Player #1
               Player #2
               Player #3
               Player #4
               Facilitator
               All players wear mismatched clothes and unusual hats. Female players wear lots of makeup in an exaggerated fashion.

(*Players 1–4 are seated at the table, with plates of chips in front of them.*)

Students enter room are seated.

PLAYER 1. (*Takes some chips from Player 3.*) Mine.

PLAYER 3. (*Takes chips from Player 1.*) No, mine!

PLAYER 2. (*Takes chips from Player 4.*) Mine.

PLAYER 3. (*Takes chips from Player 2.*) Mine.

PLAYER 4. (*Takes chips from Player 2 and stuffs them in mouth.*) Mine.

PLAYER 2. (*Takes chips from Player 1 and stuffs them in mouth.*) No, mine!

PLAYER 1. (*Takes chips from Player 4 and stuffs them in mouth.*) Mine.

PLAYER 4. (*Takes chips from Player 3.*) Mine.

PLAYER 3. (*Takes chips from Player 4 and stuffs them in mouth.*)

PLAYER 2. (*Slaps hand on table.*) I'm done. Let's play a game!

PLAYER 3. No!

PLAYER 1. Let's play games! (*Slaps hands on table.*)

PLAYER 4. Play. Let's play.

PLAYER 2. Yes, play! No chips.

PLAYER 1. Play!

PLAYER 3. Okay, play!

PLAYER 4. Clear chips. Let's play. (*Starts to pick up plates.*)

PLAYER 2. Mine! (*Grabs chips.*)

PLAYER 4. No, mine! (*Tries to grab chips.*)

PLAYER 2. Play!

PLAYER 4. (*Stacks all plates and places to the side.*)

PLAYER 1. (*Gets colored 3 × 5 cards and holds them up before placing on table.*)

PLAYER 2. Cards. Let's play.

PLAYER 3. Play.

PLAYER 4. Need dominoes.

PLAYER 3. (*Gets dominoes and places a stack in front of each player.*) Game on.

PLAYER 2. Dominoes. Game on. Let's play.

PLAYER 4. (*Grabs dominoes.*) Mine.

PLAYER 2. (*Grabs dominoes.*) Mine.

PLAYER 1. (*Grabs dominoes.*) Mine.

PLAYER 3. (*Grabs dominoes.*) Mine.

PLAYER 1. (*Takes card and holds up number on it.*) Play!

(*Each player looks at their dominoes for a side with the corresponding number of dots as the number on the card. Players who have the corresponding number give their domino to the player who drew the card.)*

PLAYER 1. (*For each domino received, Player 1 responds.*) Mine.

(*Playing continues, with the receiving person saying "Mine" when getting a domino. All players become increasingly agitated.*)

PLAYER 3. (*Jumps up and tries to grab all dominoes and stuff them in pockets.*) Mine! (*Starts to leave room.*)

PLAYERS 1, 2, and 4. (*Jump up and start pushing each other and yelling.*) Mine, mine, mine! (*All leave room following Player 3, pushing and yelling.*)

(*Facilitator enters and takes place in front.*)

PLAYER 4. (*Returns to room and gathers all the cards and remaining dominoes.*) Mine! (*Leaves room.*)

(*Players 1 and 2 return to room and gather all plates with chips.*)

PLAYER 2. Mine.

PLAYER 1. No, mine!

(*All players exit room.*)

FACILITATOR. (*Speaks to class.*) So what do you folks think about this? (*Allow time for response.*) What character traits are these players showing us? (*Allow time for response.*)

Yes, we see selfishness, greed, and envy exhibited by these players. In Luke 12:15–21 Jesus says, "Watch out! Be on your guard against all kinds of greed; a man's life does not consist in the abundance of his possessions.' And he told them this parable. 'The ground of a certain rich man produced a good crop. He thought to himself, "What shall I do? I have no place to store my crops." Then he said, "This is what I'll do. I will tear down my barns and build bigger ones, and there I will store all my grain and my goods. And I'll say to myself, 'You plenty of good things laid up for many years. Take life easy; eat, drink and be merry.'" But God said to him, "You fool! This very night your life will be demanded form you. Then who will get what you have prepared for yourself?'" This is how it will be with anyone who stores up things for himself but is not rich toward God."

Sometimes it is hard to get past the desire to have more things, even when we see we are hurting others to get it. The players were so consumed with themselves, both when eating the chips and playing the game. All they could think about was saying, "Mine." Do you ever feel you would be so much happier if you just had more of something? Do you feel you need to hold onto your stuff tightly and not share with others because it is yours? The parable in Luke, which Jesus told his disciples, illustrates how many of us want much more and will do anything to get it. Also, once we have this stuff, we just keep wanting more and more, like the man in the parable built bigger barns, not sharing or helping anyone else, being totally selfish and greedy. However, when we face God one day, we will be judged on our attitudes and actions, and we will be held accountable for how we treated others, what attitudes we had, and what words we said.

If we read further in Luke 12, we will see that God promises to take care of those who trust him. Now God does expect us to work hard and do our best at school and when we work, so we can honor him with our lives. When we cross that line of being envious of others or greedy or selfish, we sin. (*Show corresponding posters.*) Here is a dictionary definition of envy: "A feeling of discontent or ill-will because of another's advantage or possessions; resentful dislike of another who has something one desires."

The definition of greed is, "Wanting or taking all that you can get, with no thought of others' need."

If you know someone at school or church with the newest phone or electronic device, you may have some of the feelings described in these definitions. This is what the Lord is talking about in Luke 12. God wants us to be happy and content people, not jealous of others or envious. But how can we be content? God loves you and me and has provided a way to get rid of our sinful attitudes and become new people. God's only Son, Jesus, was born to live as an example for us. Jesus is perfect in every way, because he is God, and he is the way God has given us to find salvation from sins and have eternal life in heaven. John 3:16 says, "For God so loved the world that he gave his one and only son, that whoever believes in him shall not perish but have eternal life." If we believe what God says and in what he has done for us, as we are told in the Bible, and admit we are sinners and have feelings of envy and greed we talked about, we can trust in Jesus as our personal Savior and be changed. Jesus died on the cross for our sins and then rose from the dead three days later. Jesus overcame death, because he is God and was sent to earth do this loving work for us so we can be saved.

Would you close your eyes and think back to the skit we had with the players? These players were all fighting with each other because of their greed. Do you have those feelings or other sinful thoughts? Jesus came to save you and to change you. So if you believe Jesus wants to save you today, and you would like to say yes to him and trust him as your personal Savior, raise your hand so we can pray together? (*Allow response.*)

(*Say a prayer of salvation for those who respond. Allow students to open their eyes.*)

If you have made this important decision to trust Jesus as your Savior today or in the past, you are a new person. You are clean and ready to listen to Jesus speak to you through reading the Bible and prayer.

Second Corinthians 4:18 says, "While we look not at the things which are seen, but at the things which are not seen: for the things which are seen are temporal; but the things which are not seen are eternal."

You now know God will speak to you and help you grow and be more like him. Spiritual growth is invisible but real, and people will take notice of the change in your attitudes and actions. You can give Jesus all the praise for this, because he lives in you, and you will become more like him.

MIX IT UP

Set and Props—Glass bowl and table. Print enough 3 × 5 cards to give to each student with the following recipe:

> *Play Dough Recipe*
> 1 cup flour
> 1/2 cup salt
> 1 cup water
> 2 tsp. cream of tarter
> 1 tbsp. cooking oil
> Mix ingredients in a medium saucepan. Stir constantly over medium heat until sticky.
> Knead on waxed paper, adding food coloring if desired.
> Store tightly covered.

Make a batch before class and display in the glass bowl on the table.

Characters—Facilitator
> Flour Girl, wearing baggy clothes with flour sprinkled on them, hair, and face.
> Pillar of Salt, with salt glued to pieces of paper or cloth and wrap around arms, legs, and torso.
> Slick, with oil or lotion rubbed on face, arms, and hands.

Water Boy, with bottles of water tied on a cord around neck, on wrists, and around waist.

(Facilitator enters and stands in front of class.)

FLOUR GIRL. *(Enters and stands at the front.)* How can someone like me be loved by God, much less be used in doing things for him? I am not very tasty, and I make such a mess.

FACILITATOR. Flour Girl, I know you are a very necessary part of any recipe, and with the right heart, God can use you. Leviticus 2:1–2 says, "When someone brings a grain offering to the Lord, his offering is to be of fine flour. He is to pour oil on it, put incense on it and take it to Aaron's sons the priests. The priest shall take a handful of fine flour and oil, together with all the incense, and burn this as a memorial portion on the altar, an offering made by fire, an aroma pleasing to the Lord."

FLOUR GIRL. You mean God could use me as part of something that would be pleasing to him?

FACILITATOR. Yes. God loves you, and he created you just as you are—the good things about you as well as the things that cause you problems. The Bible tells us that all of us have sinned and need to find a way to remove that sin. The way God has given us is belief and trust in Jesus, his Son. Jesus died on the cross for our sins, was buried, and rose again. He will take our sins if we confess them, and Jesus will make us acceptable to God.

FLOUR GIRL. So you think Jesus would forgive my sins and let me be part of his ministry?

FACILITATOR. Yes, he will—if we admit our sins to him and place our trust in Jesus. You have a very important part in something great. You may feel plain and not wrapped in a fancy package, but God will use you for his glory. You will be very useful in the making of this play dough, and think of the hours of fun kids will have with it!

(*Four Girl steps to the side.*)

SLICK. (*Enters.*) Hi! I heard some of the things you and Flour Girl were talking about and got to thinking about any qualities I might have, besides being oily, that is.

FACILITATOR. Well, that you are. But God did create all of us for a purpose.

SLICK. I know. It's just hard to imagine anyone who would work well with me. You've heard the saying oil and water don't mix. I can't believe I would do any good being mixed up in anything.

FACILITATOR. Let me read chapter 133 in Psalms that will encourage you, Slick. "How good and pleasant it is when brothers live together in unity! It is like precious oil poured on the head, running down on Aaron's beard, down upon the collar of his robes. It is as if the dew of Hermon were falling on Mt. Zion. For them the Lord bestows his blessing, even life forevermore."

You see, Slick, oil is a unifying substance, and when you are involved in something in the right way, you can be used to hold things together.

SLICK. I just have a hard time believing that. I guess it's a problem with my faith.

FACILITATOR. When we want to be right with God, we need to believe what Jesus did for us. We need to place our faith and trust in Jesus and be thankful for the plan God has set up for us to know him.

(*Slick steps aside.*)

PILLAR OF SALT. (*Enters.*) I feel like I am going to crack before long. I feel itchy and pressured.

FACILITATOR. Why do feel this way, Pillar of Salt?

PILLAR OF SALT. I keep reading and hearing on the news that salt is so unhealthy for you and that people should stop using it. I am being disrespected. Besides that, when I am left out too long, I do not keep much of my flavor. I know God created me to add flavor but what good am I if I lose it? I feel like giving up.

FACILITATOR. Salt is used for flavor but also for many other purposes.

PILLAR OF SALT. Like what?

FACILITATOR. Through the years, salt has been used as a preservative to keep food from spoiling. Salt also has healing properties. For example, when you have a sore throat, gargle with saltwater to make it feel better. Did you know everyone needs a certain amount of salt to live? People who run, do lots of physical work, or are out in the sun lose salt from their bodies. It needs to be replenished to stay healthy.

God has created you to have a vital part in our lives. In Matthew 5:13 we read, "You are the salt of the earth. But if the salt loses its saltiness, how can it be made salty again? It is no longer good for anything, except to be thrown out and trampled by men."

PILLAR OF SALT. Now I see how important it is to keep myself in good condition and have a right relationship with God so I can be salty and useful. I will read my Bible, pray, and go to church with other believers so I can grow in Christ. I also understand how just a small amount of salt in the play dough recipe can make a difference. (*Stands to the side.*)

FACILITATOR. Hey, here comes Water Boy! How are you?

WATER BOY. (*Enters.*) I'm like I always am—necessary but ordinary. (*Slumps.*)

FACILITATOR. Well without water, where would we be?

WATER BOY. I know, but it is boring being water. Sometimes I wish I had the zing of lemonade or the punch of a cola. People would pay more attention to me.

FACILITATOR. I think you have your priorities wrong, because it is only in Jesus that we find satisfaction and purpose in living. In fact, Jesus said he is the living water. Jesus said in John 7:37, "If anyone is thirsty, let him come to me and drink. Whoever believes in me, as the scripture has said, streams of living water will flow from within him."

WATER BOY. I never thought of it like that before. I will need to confess to the Lord my sin of ungratefulness. With Jesus in my life, I can be more like him and be a big part in helping people live and even have fun doing it. Who wouldn't have fun in a swimming pool filled with water, playing with a glob of play dough, or giving people a new purpose in life through turning their heart to Jesus. (*Steps to the side.*)

FACILITATOR. No matter what we think about ourselves—whether we have self-doubts, pride, or feel we are not exciting—we need to know God created us first to have a personal relationship with Jesus. When we confess our sins and trust in Jesus as our Savior, we can have a right relationship with God and get to know him better. Would you like to make this important decision today as we pray? Please bow your heads with me. If you would like to pray and confess your sins to Jesus now as we pray, you will take the first step to a new life in Christ.

(*Say a prayer of commitment.*)

FACILITATOR. If you have prayed with me to trust Jesus as your Savior, would you tell us by raising your hand. (*Allow time for responses.*)

Now, let's look at the play dough recipe on the card you have. (*Students look at their recipe cards.*) Each item that goes into this recipe has a specific purpose. The salt, water, flour, oil, and even the small amount of cream of tarter or food coloring have something unique that combines with the other ingredients to create something useful and fun. If we know Jesus, God will use each of us, working together, to make a difference in people's lives and be pleasing to him. We may feel like we are unimportant, not talented or special, but whatever we think about ourselves does not change what God thinks and why he created you the way he did. God created you to have a relationship with Jesus and for a special purpose, so we can all work together to help others and do great things. Joy comes when we combine with others who have different abilities, like the ingredients in the play dough recipe, to accomplish something great.

(*Flower Girl, Slick, Pillar of Salt, and Water Boy all give each other high fives and shout with joy.*)

FACILITATOR. Jeremiah 29:11: "'For I know the plans I have for you,' declares the Lord, 'plans to prosper you and not harm you, plans to give you hope and a future.'"

PRIMARY COLOR AND PURITY

Props—White mat board or cardboard, stand for the board, three to four small paintbrushes, container of water to rinse brushes, small containers of red, blue, and yellow paint.

King Solomon was King David's son and was crowned king of the Israelites, God's people, when he was young. He knew he was inexperienced and needed a lot of help from God to lead the people. In faith and in pure love for God, Solomon asked the Lord to give him wisdom and a discerning heart to lead the people. God was pleased that Solomon asked for this and not for riches, a long life, or even revenge on his enemies. God did bless Solomon with wisdom, and since he was not selfish in his desires, he was given riches and honor. God instructed Solomon to be sure to obey him and to walk in God's way. You can read all about the great wisdom God gave Solomon and about the things he accomplished in Israel in 1 Kings.

Here we have some paints and brushes. (*Show them.*) How many of you have painted a picture using things like this? You know that for every color you add to another one, you create a new color. And if you add black or white, you will darken or lighten your color. Using these combinations of color, along with lighter and darker shades, a painter creates the illusion of depth, shadow, light, and interest in his work. When we talk about pure color, we are usually referring to the primary colors red, blue, and yellow. These are the colors from which all others are made.

(*Show these colors and paint a swatch of each on the board.*)

Pure colors are like our pure or primary love and devotion to God. Solomon's early years are an example of this desire to be close to God and to try to live in his will. As we continue to read about Solomon's life in 1 Kings, we see he made some bad choices and grew further from the Lord he loved. A verse in 1 Peter 1:14 says, "As obedient children do not conform to the evil desires you had when you lived in ignorance. But just as he who called you is holy, so be holy in all you do." This verse is illustrated in our paints. When we mix a primary color with another one, we create what are called secondary colors.

(*Show how red and blue make purple, blue and yellow make green, and yellow and red make orange. Be sure to wash the brushes between colors or use separate brushes to obtain the best colors.*)

Let's go back to the life of Solomon. It tells us in the Bible that Solomon took many wives of different religious beliefs. God had told the Israelites they should not marry people from places that worship idols and other gods, because this would cause them to drift away from the Lord. Nevertheless, Solomon insisted on marrying these women, and 1 Kings 11:4–8 says, "As Solomon grew old, his wives turned his heart after other gods, and his heart was not fully devoted to the Lord his God, … he followed Ashteroth the goddess of the Sidonians and Molech the detestable god of the Ammoniotes. So Solomon did evil in the sight of the Lord; he did not follow the Lord completely, as David his father had done."

If we mix our secondary colors with other secondary colors or with primary colors, we will get further from the pure primary colors.

(*Show mixed colors of orange and red to create red/orange or green with blue to create turquoise, and so on. Be sure to wash brushes between colors or use different brushes.)*

These new colors you have created are called tertiary colors, or colors of the third rank.

Solomon's downfall was gradual, and just as mixing the paint colors got us further from the pure primary colors, he got further and further from the truth of the Lord. It started affecting his life. Romans 12:2 says, "Do not conform any longer to the pattern of this world, but be transformed by the renewing of your mind." We study the Bible here at our church to learn the truths of Jesus and how he died for our sins and rose again to give us a new life. Many of you have a regular devotional time to pray and study the Bible, or time you spend studying verses to memorize. And you also have the time you spend in church services to grow in the knowledge of the Lord. However, all of us have already or will face opposition to our faith in Jesus. This opposition may be others making fun of you going to church, your beliefs, or even the way you live your life when you don't join in on doing wrong things.

If we want God's blessing on our life, we need to confess our sins and believe Jesus took our sins on himself to the cross to save us. If you want to be like the pure colors we described and like Solomon in his early life, we must continue to live in our love for Jesus, study the Scriptures, and try to obey God in our daily lives. No, we are not perfect, and that is why we can always go to Jesus and ask for forgiveness and trust that he will guide us. If you find yourself becoming further away from and less excited for the things of God, pray with me as I read this prayer of David in Psalm 51:9, 10: "Hide your face from my sins and blot out all my iniquity. Create in me a pure heart, O God, and renew a steadfast spirit within me."

PROVE IT!

Set and Props—Narrow table in front with seven red apples on it and a whiteboard on the side, with addition and subtraction tables on it.

Characters—Facilitator

        Mrs. Zigfried (teacher)

        Clown (see presession comedy), dressed in mismatched and unstylish clothes and/or glasses.

        Andrew (student)

        Penny (student)

        Emily (student)

Music—From *Cirque du Soleil,* track 10, "Ephra."

All students are dressed like ordinary students.

(*Students enter along with actors. Actors take seats among the students.*)

Presession Comedy

The clown enters, takes a look around at the apples, and then at the charts. The clown scratches head. The clown takes apples off table, puts them into pockets, and then add apples back—all while trying to do the math on his fingers. After some attempts and getting wrong answers, the clown checks out the charts and certainly can't figure them out either. (*This act should take about five minutes.*)

Finally, the clown gives up trying to add and subtract the apples and using fingers and charts. The clown just puts back the apples, but keeps one and eats it.

(*While the clown eats the apple, Mrs. Zigfried comes into class and chastises the clown for eating her arithmetic lesson for the day. Mrs. Zigfried asks the clown to leave the room and get cleaned up. Clown leaves.*)

TEACHER. Class, class (*Bangs ruler on board.*) Come to order! Class, now how many times have I told you that you are here to expand your brain cells? We are here to have fun learning math. Don't you agree that math is one of the most fun things to do? (*Points to Andrew.*)

ANDREW. Yeah, this is such a blast. (*Rolls his eyes and slouches.*)

PENNY. I love math, too!

TEACHER. Why yes, this is such fun, I can hardly sleep at night. (*Starts writing "fun with division" on the board, not listening to students.*)

EMILY. Isn't that the truth! I can't sleep well at night just thinking about coming to this class.

TEACHER. What was that, Emily? I didn't hear you.

EMILY. Mrs. Zigfried, I just said I didn't sleep well last night.

TEACHER. Oh, I'm so sorry, Emily. Today we are going to work on our division problems. Didn't I promise you we would have fun today?

EMILY AND ANDREW. (*Slouch and cover heads with hands.*) I can't believe this!

TEACHER. What did you say, Andrew? I couldn't hear you. You must sit up straight to stimulate your brain.

ANDREW. I said that I can't believe this class is so good.

TEACHER. You're such a good boy, Andrew! Now let's start. (*Writes on board, "9/3 or 9 divided by 3 equals."*) Now class, if you take the number nine and divide it by three, written like on the board, what would the answer be? (*Let someone in the class answer. If no one answers, call on Emily to answer.*) Yes, three is the answer. Very good! Why? Because if you had nine apples (*Points to the apples on the table.*) and wanted to equally divide them among three people, you would give three apples to each person. Right?

PENNY, EMILY, AND ANDREW. Yes, Mrs. Zigfried.

TEACHER. Oh, this is so exciting, isn't it, Andrew?

ANDREW. Yes, Mrs. Zigfried, so, uhum, exciting.

TEACHER. Now class, can we *prove* that nine divided by three equals three? (*Stands with hands on hips.*)

EMILY. Prove it? What more proof do we need?

TEACHER. Oh, but Emily, this is surely the most exciting part! We know the answer is three, but yes, we can even prove the answer is three by doing multiplication.

ANDREW. Oh great. First division, now multiplication! Yea, this is such fun.

TEACHER. Now Andrew, we don't need that attitude. We need to expand our brain cells. Right, Emily and Penny?

EMILY AND PENNY. Yes, Mrs. Zigfried.

TEACHER. (*Bangs ruler on podium.*) Now class, pay attention. If we divide nine apples into three equal parts (*Takes the apples on table and separates them into three groups of three.*), we have three apples in each of the three groups. Right? So to prove this, we are going to put the three groups back together. (*Moves apples back into one group.*) We ask, "How many apples do we have all together if we have three groups of three in each?" We have nine, correct? Oh, this is so much fun, I think I am going to faint!

EMILY AND ANDREW. (*Roll eyes and speak semi-softly.*) Can you believe her?

TEACHER. Yes, Andrew? I didn't hear you.

ANDREW. Oh, I just can't believe how you did that math problem.

TEACHER. Oh, Andrew, yes, isn't this so much fun? Now, getting back to the math problem, to prove this division problem we must multiply the three apples in each group by the three groups. (*Writes on board "3 × 3 equals."*) So three times three equals what, class? (*Waits for class to respond.*) Yes, nine; three multiplied by three equals nine. You are such a smart class! This is how we can prove our division problem. Well, our classtime is about up for today. Such a shame.

EMILY. Yeah, very sad.

TEACHER. But the good news is that tomorrow we are going to study how to divide fractions!

EMILY, PENNY, AND ANDREW. (*Shake heads and put hands over heads.*) Oh no!

TEACHER. And to think some people don't think it's fun to do math. I just love it! Penny, Emily, and Andrew, would you please come with me and help me set up for the pep rally this afternoon?

PENNY, EMILY, AND ANDREW. Yes, gladly!

(*All actors leave.*)

FACILITATOR. Just as we can prove things in math, as we've seen here today, we can also prove things in science. How do we do this? Yes, by experiments that prove results produced by different combinations of chemicals or conditions affecting chemicals, such as temperature. Have you ever thought about proving spiritual things? Is it wrong to try to prove God? Do we have any examples in the Bible of people trying to prove God or beliefs in God? Well, while we need to have faith in God and accept His Word and will for us, sometimes we ask for proof.

We are going to look at example of this in 1 Kings 18, where a prophet, as they called men who preached God's Word in the Bible, looked for proof of God's power to show an evil group of people who worshipped false gods. This prophet is Elijah. He was one of only one hundred prophets left at that time. They had to live in hiding because of a wicked king and queen, King Ahab and Queen Jezebel. Most of the society was very sinful and worshipped idols. They wanted to kill the prophets who preached about the true God because of their hatred of God. These people were so wicked they did not even consider that their lives and beliefs were taking them straight to hell! These people needed to see God prove who he is, and Elijah was just the man to let God work through him to do this.

First Kings 18:1–4 says, "After a long time, in the third year, the word of the

Lord came to Elijah: 'Go and present yourself to Ahab, and I will send rain on the land.' So Elijah went to present himself to Ahab. Now the famine was severe in Samaria, and Ahab had summoned Obadiah, who was in charge of his palace. (Obadiah was a devout believer in The Lord. While Jezebel was killing off the Lord's prophets, Obadiah had taken a hundred prophets and hidden them in two caves, fifty in each, and had supplied them with food and water.)"

Let us read how the one true God proved himself to people who would not decide who to worship or who had decided to worship the false god Baal. First Kings 18:20–39 says,

> So Ahab sent word throughout all Israel and assembled the prophets on Mt. Carmel. Elijah went before the people and said, "How long will you waver between two opinions? If the Lord is God, follow him, but if Baal is God, follow him." But the people said nothing. Then Elijah said to them, "I am the only one of the Lord's prophets left, but Baal has four hundred and fifty prophets. Get two bulls for us. Let them choose for themselves, and let them cut it into pieces and put it on the wood but not set fire to it. Then you call on the name of your god, and I will call on the name of the Lord. The god who answers by fire—he is God." Then all the people said, "What you say is good." Elijah said to the prophets of Baal, "Choose one of the bulls and prepare it first, since there are so many of you. Call on the name of your god, but do not light the fire." So they took the bull given them and prepared it. Then they called on the name of Baal from morning till noon. "O Baal answer us!" they shouted. But there was no response; no one answered. And they danced around the altar they had made. At noon Elijah began to taunt them. "Shout louder!" he said. "Surely he is a god! Perhaps he is deep in thought, or busy, or traveling. Maybe he is sleeping and must be awakened." So they shouted louder and slashed

themselves with swords and spears, as was their custom, until their blood flowed. Midday passed, and they continued their frantic prophesying until the time for the evening sacrifice. But there was no response, no one answered, no one paid attention. Then Elijah said to all the people, "Come here to me." They came to him and he repaired the altar of the Lord, which was in ruins. Elijah took twelve stones, one for each of the tribes descended from Jacob, to whom the word of the Lord has come saying, "Your name shall be Israel." With the stones he built an altar in the name of the Lord, and he dug a trench around it large enough to hold two seahs of seed. He arranged the wood, cut the bull into pieces and laid it on the wood. Then he said to them, "Fill four large jars with water and pour it on the offering and on the wood." "Do it again," he said, and they did it again. "Do it a third time," he ordered, and they did it the third time. The water ran down around the altar and even filled the trench. At the time of sacrifice, the prophet Elijah stepped forward and prayed: "O Lord, God of Abraham, Isaac and Israel, let it be known today that you are god in Israel and that I am your servant and have done all these things at our command. Answer me, O Lord, answer me, so these people will know, that you O Lord, are God, and that you are turning their hearts back again." Then the fire of the Lord fell and burned up the sacrifice, the wood, the stones and the soil, and licked up the water in the trench. When all the people saw this, they fell prostrate and cried, "The Lord—he is God! The Lord—he is God."

(*Explains how God created fire to burn the altar despite the amount of water that was dumped over it.*)

Just like we saw how math problems can be proved to be true, we can also prove God is real by reading his Word, the Bible. We know God is powerful enough to do miracles, as many people saw these things and believed in the reality of the true God and his Son, Jesus. While we do not need to be constantly demanding proof from God, we do need to, by faith, believe him and his wonderful gift of a Savior, who is Jesus. Jesus came to earth to save us from our sins and can do a miracle in us just like the miracle we read about. Jesus can give us the miracle forgiveness of sin and a new life!

(*Explains plan of salvation.*)

(*Close with a prayer.*)

SASQUATCH AND THE MAN ON THE MOON

Set and Props—Two different scenes placed opposite each other.

Scene 1—Interior wall of home with window in the center, old-fashioned tie-back curtains on the window. Outdated wallpaper with dated pictures on the wall. Outside scenery is a night sky with a full moon in view. In front of window is a rocking chair next to a side table lamp with books and a plate of cookies. A basket on the floor is filled with yarn and knitting needles. There is a book for Tommy and a toy rocket ship for Joey.

Scene 2—Outdoor scene of nighttime in the forest; may use silhouettes of trees. Stack of wood resembling a campfire, and a toy hunting rifle for each character.

Keep lighting at a low level.

Class will be seated in front of these sets.

Characters—Scene 1: Grandmother, dressed in old-fashioned dress and seated on the rocking chair.

Tommy, her grandson, dressed in tennis shoes, shorts, and T-shirt.

Joey, her grandson, dressed in tennis shoes, shorts, and T-shirt.

Scene 2: Melvin, a hunter, wearing hunting gear and carrying toy hunting rifle.

Edgar, a hunter, wearing hunting gear and carrying toy hunting rifle.

Facilitator

Students enter.

(*Grandmother is seated on the rocking chair, knitting and smiling at students as they enter.*)

(*Grandchildren enter and run toward grandmother.*)

JOEY. Hi, Grandma! (*Pretends to fly rocket in his hands.*) Look at my rocket. It's going to the moon!

GRANDMOTHER. Hey there, Joey. I baked some cookies. Are you hungry?

JOEY. Cookies, great! Yes, I want one. Thank you, Grandma.

GRANDMOTHER. Is your brother here, Joey?

TOMMY. (*Enters while reading a book.*) I'm here, Grandma. Did you say you had cookies?

GRANDMOTHER. I just baked them today. Help yourself. What are you reading, Tommy?

TOMMY. Oh, I'm reading about the first man who walked on the moon.

GRANDMOTHER. Do you mean the moon up there? (*Points out the window at the moon.*)

TOMMY. Yes, that's the one I'm talking about, Grandma. You know, back in the olden days—you should remember, Grandma—that Neil Armstrong was first to set foot on the moon's surface. When he stepped off the *Eagle* landing craft, he said, "That's one small step for man, one giant leap for mankind." Do you remember that, Grandma?

GRANDMOTHER. It seems like I heard something about that on television, but I don't believe it! No, that just can't be. Why, who could walk on that moon way up there? (*Points to the moon.*)

JOEY. At school, they told us about that trip the United States took to the moon, and my teacher never lies.

TOMMY. (*Shows Grandmother the book.*) Look, Grandma, here are some pictures of the first moonwalk on July 21, 1969. Grandma, were you old in 1969?

GRANDMOTHER. I wasn't always old, Tommy, and I do remember people saying there were some men up there in a rocket ship—

JOEY. (*Interrupts Grandmother.*) Like this one, Grandma (*Make rocket sounds.*), shhh, sshhh, whooooshh. (*Uses exaggerated motions to send rocket up in the air.*)

TOMMY. Put that thing down, Joey. I'm having a very important conversation with Grandma. Now Grandma, why don't you believe it when Neil Armstrong even described the dirt on the moon as like powdered charcoal?

GRANDMOTHER. I just don't see how this is even possible. Now enough of this silly talk, Tommy. Here, you go ahead and take one of my cookies, and it will make you forget about all this nonsense about the man on the moon. (*Holds out the plate of cookies to Tommy and Joey. Tommy and Joe take a cookie and start to eat it as they start to leave. Grandmother gets up and starts to exit.*)

TOMMY. Thanks, Grandma.

JOEY. Yeah, thanks, Grandma. These are really good.

GRANDMOTHER. You boys are good grandsons, even if you do have overactive imaginations.

(*The three leave.*)

FACILITATOR. (*Enters.*) Do you remember the date of the first moonwalk? (*Allow time for response.*) That's right, July 21, 1969. And who was the first astronaut to step off the lunar landing craft? (*Allow time for response.*)

Yes, Neil Armstrong was the first man to step foot on the moon, and when he did, he said something. What was that famous quote? (*Allow time for response.*) "That's one small step for man, one giant leap for mankind."

Grandma had a hard time believing the news reports that told about this historic event, because it was so different from her ordinary experiences. Unfortunately, she would not share in the pride our country had in accomplishing such a feat. The American astronauts not only flew to and landed on the moon, they also placed an American flag there to commemorate this event. But Grandma was so sure something so unusual and special could never have happened because this was beyond her understanding. Grandma has chosen not to believe something historic.

(Melvin and Edgar enter, with rifles over their shoulders. They stand near the campfire. The facilitator leaves.)

MELVIN. I told you I am not afraid of the dark. I just feel a little uneasy, that's all.

EDGAR. Melvin, it took me a long time to get you to come out here to the campsite. I think your imagination has told you something is lurking out in these dark woods. Boo! *(Makes hands quiver.)*

MELVIN. *(Jumps.)* Now stop that, Edgar. I'm a fully grown man and have my hunting rifle with me. What could I be scared of?

EDGAR. Oh, let's see. Here in the dark woods of the Pacific Northwest, where it is cold and dark, there is nothing to be afraid of. No nothing … except. Oh, never mind. What could you possibly be scared of? Ummm *(Pretends to be thinking.)*, oh, how about S-A …

MELVIN. That's enough! *(Stomps foot.)* You stop it right now, Edgar! Maybe you should be more cautious. You can't be too careful, you know.

EDGAR. Careful that old Native American legends come to life and come out of the wood to get you? Grrrrr. *(Grabs at Melvin.)*

MELVIN. Get off me, or I'm going to hit you over the head! I'm going home right now!

EDGAR. Go ahead. Walk back to the truck, down that dark, lonely, cold trail. I'll come when I feel like it. But don't let that—er—creature see you. He may not have had supper yet. *(Laughs.)*

MELVIN. You quit telling me what to do. I don't believe in those old stories about that … that … that thing!

EDGAR. Oh well, there's no one here except us in the middle of these dark woods—except maybe, no that couldn't be. S-A-S-Q …

MELVIN. (*Holds up hand.*) Don't you say it. Just don't say it! It will bring us bad luck on this kind of night. I'm leaving with you or without you. I hope he eats your head first and then chews you up and spits your smelly body out!

EDGAR. Don't be such a baby, Melvin. It's too cold out here. Let's go back to the cabin.

(*Edgar and Melvin start to exit.*)

MELVIN. Just stop it, will you?

EDGAR. Sasquatch, oh Sasquatch, where are you? Did you eat supper yet? (*Looks around.*)

MELVIN. Shhshhshh. You've got a big mouth, you know that?

EDGAR. Baby. (*Points at Melvin.*)

FACILITATOR. (*Enters.*) Sasquatch is the name for a large, hairy, ape-like man that, according to legend, hides in the forests of the Pacific Northwest and preys on various animals and people. This old story has been handed down from generation to generation and says that few people have actually seen this creature. This creature leaves its mark, however, by a trail of large footprints, which explains its other nickname, Big Foot. We don't know if this creature is real, but he lives in the imaginations of many people who fear him and don't want to be alone in the big woods, especially at night.

Sometimes we are presented with things we have trouble believing because, like Grandma and the man on the moon, these things are different from our normal experiences, and we choose not to believe so we don't deal with them. There are other times when, like the case of our two hunters, we are controlled by the idea or fear something is there that probably isn't. This fear comes from people telling us exaggerated stories or not being truthful. Perhaps a long time ago someone saw a large bear and told the story, which was passed down from generation to generation and exaggerated with each telling, until the bear became Sasquatch.

We have an account in the Bible about Jesus and the difficulty Thomas, one of the disciples, had in believing the truth. We read in the previous chapters about Jesus' death on the cross, his burial in the tomb, and his resurrection three days later. God tells us in the Bible that he sent Jesus forgive our sins on the cross if we just admit and confess our sinners. You know, all of us were born sinners and need a way of forgiveness. God gave us Jesus to be that way if we believe the truth of what he has done and trust him as our Savior. John 3:16, 17 says, "For God so loved the world that he gave his only begotten Son, that whosoever believes in him shall not perish but have eternal life. For god did not send his son into the world to condemn the world, but to save the world through him."

After Jesus rose from the dead, the Bible tells us he showed himself to many people before going to heaven to be with God the Father. Let me read what happened after Jesus came out of the tomb. John 20:19–30 says, "On the evening of that first day of the week, when the disciples were together, with the doors locked for fear of the Jews, Jesus came and stood among them and said 'Peace to you!' After he said this he showed them his hands at his side. The disciples were overjoyed when they saw the Lord … Now Thomas one of the Twelve was not with the disciples when Jesus came. So the other disciples told him 'We have seen the Lord!' But he said to them, 'Unless I see the nail marks in his hands and put my finger where the nails were, and put my hand into his side I will not believe it.' A week later his disciples were in the house again, and Thomas was with them. Though the doors were locked, Jesus came and stood among them and said, 'Peace be with you.' Then he said to Thomas, 'Put your finger her; see my hands Reach out your hand and put it into my side. Stop doubting and believe!' Thomas said to him, 'My Lord and my God!' Then Jesus told him, 'because you have seen me, you have believed, blessed are those who have not seen and yet have believed.'"

Thomas knew that Jesus' death on the cross was real and that nails were driven into his hands and feet, and a spear was thrust into his side. because he personally witnessed this. The trouble that Thomas had was that he could not believe Jesus was still alive, that he truly was God. Like the grandmother who would not believe the fact of the moon landing, Thomas would not believe Jesus was alive when the other disciples and others told him they had seen him. Thomas had a lack of faith. God tells us to possess faith in him and his Son, Jesus, and our lives will be changed by the power of the Holy Spirit. We need to know what is real and believe it. Then we need to put that belief into action and trust our lives to the Lord.

Unlike the hunters who had a belief in something that was probably not real, we know from God's Word, the Bible, that Jesus' life, death, and resurrection is true. We do not have to doubt, and we can make a decision to believe in Jesus to save us. If you believe what Jesus did for you and confess your sins, he will forgive your sins and give you faith to trust. Jesus wants to save you and change your life; he wants to give you a hope for the future. Would you take that step of faith today as we pray together?

(*Say a prayer of commitment.*)

With your eyes still closed, will those of you who placed your trust in Jesus during that prayer please stand? We do not need to be ashamed of what God has done in our lives. (*Allow response, and let students who stood be seated.*)

You have had faith and believed without Jesus standing here physically. In the Scripture we read Jesus told Thomas that we will be blessed for making this decision. God will bless you through the peace of his Holy Spirit today for believing.

(*Say a prayer of thanks.*)

STRONG ROOTS—GREAT SHOOTS

Set and Props—Table and four chairs. Four pans of different types of soil: gravel, hard clay, turf with weeds, and potting soil. Place on a separate table near the entrance of room so students pass this and observe when they enter.

Characters—Facilitator

> Green plant, dressed in different shades of green and use green face paint on your face and hands, spray hair green or contrasting color.
>
> Wilted flower, dressed in drab clothes with dirt or smudges on them and worn and torn shoes. Cut-out flower shape of posterboard, with a face hole cut out. Curl and tear edges of petals to look unattractive. Tousle hair and smudge dirt on hands.

(*Enter students, who walk past and observe soil types and then are seated.*)

FACILITATOR. (*Enters and stands in front of class to read Scripture.*) Matthew 13:3–9: "Then he told them many things in parables saying; 'A farmer went out to show his seed, as he was scattering his seed, some fell along the path and the birds came and ate it up. Some fell on rocky places where it did not have much soil. It sprang up quickly because the soil was shallows; but when the sun came up, the plants were scorched, and they withered because they had no root. Still other seed fell among thorns, which grew up and choked the plants. Still other seed fell on good soil where it produced a crop—a hundred, sixty or thirty times what was sown.'"

Matthew 13: 16–23: "Listen to what the parable of the sower means: 'when anyone hears the message about the kingdom and does not understand it, the evil one comes and snatches away what was sown in his heart. This is the seed down along the path. The one who received the seed that fell on rocky places is the man who hears the word and at once receives it with joy. But since he has no root, he lasts only a short time. When trouble or persecution comes because of the word, he quickly falls away. The one who received the seed that fell among the thorns is the man who hears the word, but the worries of this life and the deceitfulness of wealth choke it, making it unfruitful. But the one who received the seed that fell on good soil is the man who hears the word and understands it. He produces a crop, yielding a hundred, sixty or thirty times what was sown.'"

(*Facilitator stands to side or exits.*)

GREEN PLANT. (*Enters energetically, smiling and greeting students.*) Hi, everybody! How are you doing? Today is a great day, isn't it? The day has been sunny and warm, after a nice refreshing rain yesterday. I just feel great. (*Looks as Wilted flower enters.*) Oh, hi there, flower!

WILTED FLOWER. (*Enters room, slouched, head down, and feet dragging.*) What did you say?

GREEN PLANT. I said, "Hi, how are you doing?"

WILTED FLOWER. Not so great. This sun is so hot, it just wears me out.

GREEN PLANT. Wasn't the rain yesterday just what you needed to feel better?

WILTED FLOWER. No, all that wet stuff pounded down on me and just washed me out from the bottom up. I can't get my footing! (*Stumbles around.*)

GREEN PLANT. Well, my roots just drank up that moisture and made me firm up all over. Look at this! (*Gets down on the floor, does some pushups, and then stands.*)

WILTED FLOWER. I don't have enough energy to do all that. Why, just look at me. (*Slouches down further.*) My root system just never got established, and I can barely support my weight. It seems like the nutrients in the soil are not getting up to my petals.

GREEN PLANT. It may be that bad soil that you grew up in. When I looked at that hard-packed soil, I couldn't even imagine how you grew as much as you have.

WILTED FLOWER. I know. God blessed you with nice fertile soil that had many nutrients in it and was nice and soft for your roots to grow deep and strong. I just don't know how I can keep going.

GREEN PLANT. I have an idea. If it's not too late, maybe we can get your roots into some good soil, where you can rest up and get enough nutrition and water. If you did this, maybe your root system would grow, and you would feel stronger and improve your petals.

WILTED FLOWER. That's an idea. I just can't think right now. I've got a headache.

GREEN PLANT. (*Puts arm around Wilted flower and begins to exit.*) Let me help you find some good ground. I think there may be some over here. Come with me.

WILTED FLOWER. Oh, all right. Maybe you can help me.

FACILITATOR. (*Enters to front of class.*) As you can see, students, it is so important that we establish a good root system in our lives, so we can grow and thrive instead of die out. When we talk about our physical bodies, we know that to have strong bodies and good health we need to eat the right foods and get exercise. When we were babies, our parents made sure we had milk and nutritious food so our bodies would grow correctly, with strong bones and good skin and hair. This is like the root system we are talking about in plants and tress. If you plant a seed, you must do the right things to help it grow. First, you need to plant the seed in good soil and then water it. You need to protect the seed as it takes root in the soil, so the roots will become deep and strong. In doing these things, and with time, a healthy plant will grow.

When you entered the room, you saw different types of soil. As we read the parable of the sower in Matthew, we remember that seeds cannot develop correctly in bad soil. The symbolism of this parable is that our belief in salvation through Jesus is by faith, and this seed of faith that is planted must also be taken care of in a proper environment for growth and strength to take place. The parable also explains the importance of a strong and deep root system, spiritually speaking. Jeremiah 17: 7–8 says, "But blessed is the man who trusts in the Lord, whose confidence is in him. He will be like a tree planted by the water that sends out its roots by the stream. It does not fear when heat comes; its leaves are always green. It has no worries in a year of drought and never fails to bear fruit."

All of you are here in this class to learn about the things of God, and many of you attend other classes and churches as well. Each of you has the potential to plant the seed of faith—called salvation—in Jesus

Christ and the opportunity to learn more and grow in good soil. It is up to you to make sure you put yourself in the correct environment and do the right things to grow and spread deep spiritual roots. If you believe Jesus is the Son of God, that he died on the cross for your sins, and that he rose from the dead three days later, you can place your trust in Jesus as your personal Savior. You can plant the seed of faith in Jesus in your life and decide to do the things that will help you grow. Find good teachers and preachers, read your Bible, pray and tell others about the change that has taken place in your life since you were saved. In doing this, your roots will grow and spread like the tree planted beside the water. Your spiritual life will grow like this tree, and your life will bear good fruit if you take care of your spiritual life and try to please the Lord.

Would you bow your heads and close your eyes? Think about the parable and the other Scriptures we have read together. Then ask yourself if you have planted that first seed of faith in Christ Jesus. Trusting Jesus as your Savior is the most important decision you will make in your life, because it is an eternal decision. Do you think God's Holy Spirit is speaking to you right now? If so, would you respond to Jesus by raising your hand high? (*Allow time for response.*)

Let's pray together. You may put your hands down.

(*Say a prayer of salvation. After the prayer, ask students to open their eyes.*)

Today, some of you have made a decision to follow Jesus. Your sins are forgiven, and you will experience a big change in your life. Some of you have already trusted Christ as your Savior and will want to know him better and grow in your faith. Let me read to you Ephesians 3:17: "I pray that you being rooted and established in love, may have power, together with all the saints, to grasp how wide and long and high and deep is the love of Christ, and to know this love that surpasses knowledge—that you may be filled to the measure of all the fullness of God."

Jesus loves you and has given his life for our sins, and we will go to heaven when we die. Only Jesus' great love for us allows us to be saved. To be like that tree Jeremiah describes, you need to stay rooted in good soil, in the things of God. You need to do things that build your faith, such as go to church, read your Bible, pray, and make friends with others who share your faith. Listen to God when you spend time in the Word, and stay close to Jesus. Make wise choices that will please God. Do these things, and you will grow deep roots and produce fruit in your life.

TRAUMA CENTER RESCUE

Set and Props—Set up six tables around the room to simulate a trauma center. Place white sheets on each table, where patients will lie. May string white sheets from ceiling to create curtain cubicles. May have IV trees or any old, unused things from a hospital storage room to place around room to give it an authentic atmosphere. Play a recording of sirens, talking, and so on in the background.

Characters —Doctor in lab coat with stethoscope.
        2 Nurses in scrubs.
        Patient #1, put black, blue, and red makeup on finger—dislocated finger.
        Patient #2, put ice pack on jaw—broken jaw.
        Patient #3, nonresponsive—ruptured aneurysm.
        Patient #4, patch on eye—corneal abrasion.
        Patient #5, bandage around foot and crutches—fractured metatarsal.
        Patient #6, hands clutching chest—myocardial infarction (heart attack).

(All patients should be in place on the tables except patient #6, who will enter after students enter. When the students enter, the doctor and nurses will escort them from patient to patient as the lesson progresses.)

PATIENT #1. (*Moans in pain and holding hand.*) Hey, Doc, this really hurts. Can you do something for me?

DOCTOR. What seems to be the problem today, sir?

PATIENT #1. It's my finger, Doc. I think it's broken. It really hurts.

DOCTOR. Let's take a look at it, okay? (*Gently takes hand and examines finger.*) Can you bend your finger at the joint?

PATIENT. I don't know, Doc. Just fix it.

DOCTOR. We can fix it right up. Nurses, we'll need a splint and some tape and bandages. You can start cleaning his hand.

NURSES. Okay, we'll get started. (*Nurses and doctor wok on patient's hand, putting on a splint and wrapping it.*)

DOCTOR. Students, I want you to remember that this dislocated finger reminds us of what the Lord tells us in Proverbs 3:5, 6: "Trust in the Lord with all your heart and lean not on your own understanding; in all your ways acknowledge him, and he will make your paths straight." You know that when we get off track spiritually and do not stick close to God and do not trust Jesus, our lives become like this disjointed finger; things do not work right. We re-set the finger to heal properly, just as we need to trust in Jesus and follow his teachings so our path in life will be straight, and we function correctly. Now we need to move on, class.

(*Turns back to patient.*) There you go. You should be good as new in a short time. (*Doctor leads students to patient #2 and directs them to stand around the table.*)

PATIENT #2. (*As doctor, nurses, and students enter area, the patient tries* to talk, making grunts and sounds. Patient keeps pointing to his jaw and opening mouth.)

DOCTOR. Hello, I am the doctor and would like to help you today. With me are nurses and some students. (Doctor gently feels patient's jaw.) I understand you have a broken jaw. Have you been in a fight? (Patient #2 nods.)

Nurses, we need to prep this patient, and I will arrange for surgery, as his jaw needs to be taken care of as soon as possible. (Turns to patient.) I need your consent and then I will arrange for a surgeon to speak with you about fixing your jaw. Does that sound good? (Patient #2 nods.)

Nurses, please place an ice pack on this patient's jaw while he waits. (Nurses place an ice pack on his jaw.)

Matthew 12:34–36 tells us, "For out of the overflow of the heart the mouth speaks. The good man brings good things out of the good stored up in him, and the evil man brings evil things out of the evil storied up in him, but I tell you that men will have to give an account on the day of judgment for every careless word they have spoken." We must be sure our soul is right with God, so when we speak to others, what we say will build them up and help them, not tear them down. Our mouth will be broken by careless words spoken, and we will be judged by what we say. On to the next patient.

(Doctor, nurses, and students proceed to patient #3.)

(Doctor lifts eyelids, one at a time, to examine the patient and then takes blood pressure and listens to heart with the stethoscope.) Oh my, this patient is in grave danger, not responsive. I believe he may have an aneurysm, but to be sure, we will need to send him up to take a CAT scan and an MRI to evaluate.

NURSE #1. Yes, Doctor, right away. (Nurses pull sheet up to chin and place arms of patient at the side to prepare for transport.)

DOCTOR. (Whispers.) Students, this patient will need a lot of prayers as he is not responsive. The Bible tells us about those who are not responsive to the Gospel, even when they are told how to be saved. Ephesians 4:17–19 says, "So I tell you this, and insist on it in the Lord, that you must no longer live as the gentiles do, in the futility of their thinking. They are darkened in their understanding and separated from the life of God because they are ignorance that is in them due to the hardening of their hearts. Having lost all sensitivity, they have given themselves over to sensuality so as to indulge in every impurity." Be careful, class, to listen and be aware of what God is saying to you so you do not become hardened by the world.

Okay, now let's see what is going on at the next table. (Takes students to patient #4.)

(Speaks to patient #4.) How are you today?

PATIENT #4. Not so good, doctor. They put this patch on my eye, because it hurts so bad. (Points to the patch.)

DOCTOR. Let me take a look. (Gently lifts the patch and looks.) When did you start to have this eye pain?

PATIENT #4. Well, Doc, I was cutting some tree branches down, and a limb brushed against my face. Suddenly I couldn't see out of this eye, and it hurt so bad.

DOCTOR. Cutting down trees sure is dangerous and hard work. Let me take another look. (Takes another look at the eye.) Nurses, I think we need to write a prescription for some topical cream for this patient's eye, to be applied twice daily, because he has a corneal abrasion.

(*Speaks to patient.*) All of us have had the experience of looking at something that would not be pleasing to God. We read in Matthew 6:22–23, "The eye is the lamp of the body. If your eyes are good, your whole body will be full of light. But if your eyes are bad your whole body will be full of darkness. If then the light within you is darkness, how great is that darkness." Be careful of what you look at!

We are running out of time, so let's go see our last patient. (*Moves class to patient #5.*)

NURSE #2. Hello, it looks like you had an accident.

NURSE #1. What happened?

PATIENT #5 – (*Groans and holds leg.*) My foot! I can't believe I was so stupid to walk on that rickety old floor.

DOCTOR. You were in an old house?

PATIENT #5. Yes, I was looking through it to see if I might be able to remodel it and sell it. I fell right through the floor and broke my foot. Man, it really hurts.

DOCTOR. (*Examines foot.*) The chart says you have a fractured metatarsal. I'm sure it does hurt. I see you've already had a bandage put on and some crutches. That is good. I think your foot will heal nicely with time. In the meantime, we will give you some medication to manage the pain.

Students, Psalm 119:133 tells us, "Direct my footsteps according to your word; let no sin rule over me." When we seek God for forgiveness, we do so knowing Jesus died on the cross for our sins, and because of him, we can be saved. We are all born sinners and need a savior, Jesus is the Savior.

PATIENT #6. (*Enters room clutching chest and in great pain.*) Help me, help me! My heart! Something is wrong! (*Falls to floor.*)

DOCTOR. (*Gathers students around patient.*) Let's get this patient up on a table. (*Students help lift patient onto table. The doctor listens to patient's chest. Turns to speak to nurses.*) Yes, it's what I thought, a probable myocardial infarction. Take the patient immediately to cardiac care for a full workup. I'll call the cardiac specialist.

(*Nurses lead students away from tables.*)

DOCTOR. You know, students, all of us must realize it is so important to have a healthy heart. This organ pumps blood through the body and needs to be in good working order. While our physical heart is strengthened with exercise and healthy eating, even more important is the health of our soul or spiritual heart. Have you ever thought about the health of your soul or spiritual heart? Is your heart so sick with sin that you are in danger of a heart attack? What would happen if your soul failed? The Bible tells us that when we die, we will spend eternity in one or two places: heaven or hell. I want you to know today that when you die, you will be in heaven with Jesus forever. We read in Romans 10:9–10, "That if you confess with your mouth, 'Jesus is Lord,' and believe in your heart that God raised him from the dead, you will be saved. For it is with your heart that you believe and are justified, and it is with your mouth that you confess and are saved."

Will you decide to protect your soul today and trust Jesus as your Savior? To have a healthy life on earth and in eternity, you can make this decision to be saved now. Will you pray with me?

(*Say a prayer of commitment.*)

TRUSTING GOD'S PLAN OF CARE

Set and Props—Painted scenery of the interior of an Egyptian palace with window openings looking out on vistas of desert, palms, pyramids, and the Nile. For each servant, a feather fan on a long pole. There are various chairs, pedestals, and palms in keeping with Egyptian motif. There should be a podium for storyteller.

Characters—Joseph, dressed in a decorative robe, sandals, and Egyptian-style headband.

2 Servants, dressed in plain robes and sandals.

Storyteller, dressed in a decorative robe or top and pants.

(Servants stand at attention with fans at their sides as class enters and during storytelling. Storyteller stands near the podium and greets children and directs them to seats. Storyteller then takes place behind podium. Joseph is behind the set and controls the soft harp and flute music CD.)

STORYTELLER. In the book of Genesis, we read that Jacob became an important leader of God's people. He had twelve sons, and Joseph was the next-to-youngest son as well as his favorite. (May comment that it is not a good idea for parents to play favorites with their children, but this was a factor in this story.) Jacob gave Joseph a beautiful coat of many colors, and the brothers became very jealous of him. One day the brothers were away from their house, tending sheep in the pasture. They saw Joseph in the distance, coming to meet up with them. Genesis 37:19 says, "They plotted to kill him and said to each other, 'Look here comes that dreamer!'" The plan was to kill him and throw his body into a pit. But one of his brothers, Reuben, came to the rescue and told the others they should not carry the guilt of murder on themselves but, instead, just throw Joseph into the pit alive. As the brothers were debating what to do with Joseph, a caravan of traders came along, and the brothers came up with the idea of selling Joseph to them. They kept his special coat and spread goat blood all over it to make it look like an animal killed Joseph. The brothers went home to their father and showed him Joseph's bloody coat. Jacob was so upset, believing his son was dead and mourned his loss. Meanwhile, the traders took Joseph to Egypt, where they sold him as a servant to Potiphar, the pharaoh's captain of the guard.

Even in these bad circumstances, Joseph trusted God. Rather than being a coward, Joseph showed courage and faith in God in the face of danger. Genesis 39:2, 3 says, "The Lord was with Joseph and he prospered, and he lived in the house of his Egyptian master. When the master saw that the Lord was with him and that the Lord gave him success in everything he did, Joseph found favor in his eyes and became his attendant. Joseph put him in charge of his household, and he entrusted to his care everything he owned."

(*Storyteller sits, and Joseph enters. Servants lightly fan Joseph.*)

JOSEPH. I worked very hard for the pharaoh and prayed that God would help me be brave, even though I was homesick for my family. God took care of me and helped me learn the Egyptian language and culture.

One day, Potiphar's wife tried to get me to do something that was wrong. I told her I would never do anything to disobey God and cheat on my master. The woman was very angry and told a lie about me to her husband, which got me thrown into prison. Again, I was in a very bad situation, but I remembered God love me and will take care of me in his time and in his way, not mine.

How many of you have had bad things done to you or have had people tell a lie about you? How did that make you feel? Matthew 6:14 says, "For if you forgive men when they sin against you, your heavenly Father will forgive you also." Let's pray right now, and ask God to help us forgive those who have done wrong to us.

(Pray for us to remember God loves us and will help us through hard times.)

(Servants stop fanning and stand. Joseph exits, and the storyteller comes to the podium.)

STORYTELLER. One day Pharaoh's butler and baker were thrown into the same prison where Joseph was. Both of these men had dreams and wanted to find someone who could tell them what they meant. Joseph prayed to God for wisdom, and God gave Joseph the ability to interpret their dreams. Joseph interpreted the butler's dream to mean he would go back to work for Pharaoh. Genesis 40:14 tells us what Joseph said to the butler when he left jail to go back to his job: "But when all goes well with you, remember me and show me kindness; mention me to Pharaoh and get me out of this prison." However, when the butler left prison, he forgot all about Joseph.

(The storyteller sits, and Joseph enters. Servants begin to fan Joseph.)

JOSEPH. Two long years went by, and I was still locked up. Then one night Pharaoh had a dream, and no one could tell him what it meant. That is when the butler suddenly remembered me and told Pharaoh I could possibly help. "Bring Joseph to me," Pharaoh said. After Pharaoh told me about his dream, I prayed to God for wisdom. God gave me the meaning of the dream, which I told to Pharaoh. He was so pleased he said, "God is with you, so I will make you second in command in all of Egypt." I prayed for God's help and for wisdom in running Egypt. You can see God was still providing for me and that he cared for me in more ways than I could have ever imagined.

Have you ever had the thought that God might have forgotten about you when you were having a very bad experience? Do you remember a bad time you or your family have gone through? In 1 Peter 5:6, 7 it says, "Humble yourselves, therefore, under God's mighty hand, that he may lift you up in due time. Cast all you care upon him because he cares for you." Let's pray right now, and ask the Lord to give us patience and wisdom when we go through a hard time.

(*Say a prayer of thanksgiving for God's wisdom and for struggles that produce character in us.*)

(*Servants stop fanning and stand. Joseph exits and the storyteller goes to the podium.*)

STORYTELLER. Do you remember us talking about Joseph's brothers and his father, Jacob? They did not know where Joseph was or that he was a ruler in Egypt. The Bible tells us a severe famine was experienced in all the surrounding countries, including Egypt and where Jacob's family was. Over the years, God had given Joseph special wisdom to save large quantities of grain and food and to tell to others during the upcoming famine. This storage of food put Egypt in a very good position to sell food to other countries during this severe famine. Twice, Joseph's family ran out of food and decided to go to Egypt to buy some. You can read about this in more detail in the book of Genesis.

The second time they went to Egypt for food, Joseph's family brought their youngest brother, Benjamin. When Joseph's brothers arrived, they did not recognize Joseph, but Joseph recognized them. He did not let them know he knew who they were. Joseph looked closely at his brothers to see if they were still mean. He sold them grain and put it in sacks for traveling. Joseph also placed a silver cup into Benjamin's sack with a special purpose. When the brothers had traveled a short way, Joseph sent a servant to stop them. The servant found the cup in Benjamin's sack and took him back to Joseph's palace. The other brothers, upset about the mix-up, followed them back. "Please sir," my brother said to Joseph, "our father, is very old. He loves Benjamin very much. Let me take Benjamin's place."

(*Storyteller sits down, and Joseph enters. Servants stay at attention.*)

JOSEPH. I finally knew my brothers had changed, and I forgave them. I then told them I was their brother from long ago. My brothers became so afraid I would punish them, but I told them not to be afraid, because though they meant to do evil to me, God used the bad situation for good. For one thing, God placed me in this position to help them and others through this terrible famine. Then I asked them to hurry home and bring our father and the whole family to Egypt to live. I was so happy my family came to Egypt during this time of famine. The forgiveness God showed me I was able to show my brothers.

Can you think of a time you chose to forgive someone? Did that act of forgiveness create good in that situation? God tells us in Romans 8:28, "And we know that all things work together for good to those that love him." We do not know what problems we will face in our lives. The story of Joseph shows us the abuse others can give us, we can see the lies others can tell about us, and we can see just how rough life can be. You may have problems at home or at school. We may have problems with learning difficult subjects or not be good at music, sports, or art. But God knows each one of us and each one of our situations. We know we will face problems, some bigger and some smaller, but we can also be sure God loves us. John 3:16 says, "For God so loved the world that whosoever believeth in him shall have eternal life." God sent Jesus into the world to forgive our sins through his death on the cross and his resurrection from the tomb. You can say yes to Jesus today and find forgiveness for your sins and have a new life. When you find the forgiveness for your sins that Jesus gives you, you can also forgive others—like I did my brothers. You can have this change in your life today and bring change to others if you will make the right decision.

(*Say a prayer of salvation.*)

TWO HEADS ARE BETTER THAN ONE

Sets and Props—A card table, covered with a tablecloth, is in front of the students. On the card table are two glass heads, large doll heads, or glass jars with faces painted on them. Nine colors of paper, cut into strips (two per color), to print comments on are on one head, and corresponding verses are on in the other head.

Character—Teacher

TEACHER. Did you ever hear that two heads are better than one? This is true if what is in the second head is better or more helpful than what is in the first head. Have you ever thought of something and then realized what you thought wasn't really such a good thought or idea? Sometimes the Devil wants to trip us up and get us into trouble with bad thoughts. God is good to us, however, and if we just look into his Word—the Bible—he can bring our thoughts and attitudes into line with what is right and good for our lives. *If we know Jesus as our Savior, we do many things in our lives, but the most important thing is to study God's Word and let it change us.* We are going to look at some thoughts that may have been in your head, just like this one (*Shows head with comments on it.*) and then we will see how God's Words compare.

(Shows second head.)

(*Draws a comment from "my head" comments and read. You may then discuss. Draws the corresponding color sheet from "God's head" and read. Continue until all comments are used.*) _

My Head. I feel so stupid in my schoolwork. I think I'll just forget about it and have a good time.

God's Head. Proverbs 10:14: "Wise men store up knowledge but the mouth of a fool invites ruin."

(*Allow time for discussion.*)

My Head. My parents are divorced, and I don't see very many good marriages. I don't know if I want to get married when I grow up.

God's Head. Matthew 19:6: "Haven't you read, that at the beginning the Creator made them male and female and said—For this reason a man shall leave his father and mother and be united with his wife, and they will become one flesh so they are no longer two but one. Therefore what God has joined together let man not separate."

(*Allow time for discussion.*)

My Head. What good is memorizing all these verses in the Bible anyway?

God's Head. Proverbs 22:17–20: "Pay attention and listen to the sayings of God. Apply your heart to what I teach, for it is pleasing when you keep them in your heart and have all of them ready on your lips. So that your trust may be in the Lord, I teach you today, ever you. Have I not written sayings for you? Sayings of counsel and knowledge, teaching you true and reliable words, so you can give sound answers to him who sent you?"

(*Allow time for discussion.*)

My Head. I don't have friends and don't care anyway!

God's Head. John 14:13: "Greater love has no man than this, that he lays down his life for his friends." Proverbs 18:24: "A man of many companions comes to ruin, but there is a friend who sticks closer than a brother."

(*Allow time for discussion.*)

My Head. I want peace for myself and the world, but I do not know how to find it.

God's Head. John 16:33: "I have told you these things, so that you may have peace, in this world you will have trouble. But take heart! I have overcome the world!"

(*Allow time for discussion.*)

My Head. I am old enough to not listen to my parents. They are always on my back!

God's Head. Ephesians 6:1, 2: "Children obey your parents in the Lord, for this is right. Honor your father and your mother—which is the first commandment with a promise—that it may go well with you and that you may enjoy long life on the earth."

(*Allow time for discussion.*)

My Head. All this stuff to do in the schoolbooks— don't feel like doing it, because I want to be doing fun stuff.

God's Head. Proverbs 1:7: "The fear of the Lord is the beginning of knowledge, but fools despise wisdom and discipline."

(*Allow time for discussion.*)

My Head. Sometimes I feel like hurting myself. I'm not worth much of anything to my parents, friends, or teachers.

God's Head. Psalm 139:13–16. "For you created my innermost being, you knit me together in my mother's womb. I praise you because I am fearfully and wonderfully made; your works are wonderful I know this full well. My frame was not hidden from you when I was made in the secret place. When I was woven together within the depth of the earth, your eyes saw my unformed body, all the days ordained for me were written in your book before one of them came to be."

(Allow time for discussion.)

My Head. I want to be in the cool group and be popular. I don't care that they do not follow the rules. It's important to me to fit in.

God's Head. Matthew 7:13: "Wide is the gate and broad is the road that leads to destruction and many enter through it. But small is the gate and narrow the road that leads to life and only few find it."

(Allow time for discussion.)

*(Teacher addresses students.)*You have heard that things in life that are worthwhile may not be easy to obtain. Yes, we must put forth thought, effort, and discipline to be the best version of us we can be! God has designed it this way, but the good news is we have someone to help us do this. Who? Jesus, the Son of God, came into this world to give us an example of how to live and think. He also came to die for our sins and rose again to show us he is truly God. Jesus can be your best friend and Savior. He loves you. If you confess your sins to him and trust him as your Savior, he will direct your life, give you purpose, and enable you to do so many things you haven't thought possible! He will change your life!

(Ask for commitments. Conclude with a prayer.)